Thank you for all you do for our children!

Sincerely, CALSA Board of Directors

CALSA Mission:

The California Association of Latino Superintendents and Administrators (CALSA) is a community of diverse educational leaders skilled in addressing the needs of Latino/a students and dedicated to increasing the number of highly effective Latino/a administrators.

GOOD
LEADERS
ASK
GREAT
QUESTIONS

Books by Dr. John C. Maxwell
Can Teach You How to Be a REAL Success

Relationships

25 Ways to Win with People

Becoming a Person of Influence

Encouragement Changes Everything

Ethics 101

Everyone Communicates, Few Connect

The Power of Partnership

Relationships 101

Winning with People

Attitude

Attitude 101

The Difference Maker

Failing Forward

How Successful People Think

Sometimes You Win, Sometimes You Learn

Success 101

Thinking for a Change

The Winning Attitude

Equipping

The 15 Invaluable Laws of Growth

The 17 Essential Qualities of a Team Player

The 17 Indisputable Laws of Teamwork

Developing the Leaders Around You

How Successful People Grow

Equipping 101

Make Today Count

Mentoring 101

My Dream Map

Partners in Prayer

Put Your Dream to the Test

Running with the Giants

Talent Is Never Enough

Today Matters

Your Road Map for Success

Leadership

The 21 Irrefutable Laws of Leadership, 10th Anniversary Edition

The 21 Indispensable Qualities of a Leader

The 21 Most Powerful Minutes in a Leader's Day

The 360 Degree Leader

Developing the Leader Within You

The 5 Levels of Leadership

Go for Gold

Good Leaders Ask Great Questions

How Successful People Lead

Leadership 101

Leadership Gold

Leadership Promises for Every Day

GOOD
LEADERS
═ ASK ═
GREAT
QUESTIONS

YOUR FOUNDATION FOR
SUCCESSFUL LEADERSHIP

JOHN C.
MAXWELL

CENTER
STREET

NEW YORK BOSTON NASHVILLE

The author is represented by Yates & Yates, LLP, Literary Agency, Orange, California.

Center Street
Hachette Book Group
1290 Avenue of the Americas
New York, NY 10104

centerstreet.com

Printed in the United States of America

RRD-C

First edition: October 2014

10 9 8 7 6 5 4

Center Street is a division of Hachette Book Group, Inc.
The Center Street name and logo are trademarks of Hachette Book Group, Inc.

The Hachette Speakers Bureau provides a wide range of authors for speaking events. To find out more, go to www.HachetteSpeakersBureau.com or call (866) 376-6591.

The publisher is not responsible for websites (or their content) that are not owned by the publisher.

Library of Congress Cataloging-in-Publication Data

Maxwell, John C.
   Good leaders ask great questions : your foundation for successful leadership / John C. Maxwell. — First Edition.
      pages cm
   Summary: "In GOOD LEADERS ASK GREAT QUESTIONS, John C. Maxwell delves into the process of becoming a successful leader by examining how questions can be used to advantage. What are the questions leaders should ask themselves? What questions should they ask members of their team? He then responds to the toughest problems leaders have presented to him. Using social media, Maxwell offered the floor to followers with unanswered questions about what it takes to achieve their professional best, and selected seventy questions on the most popular topics, including: —How can I discover my unique purpose as a leader? —What is the most effective daily habit that any leader should develop? —How do you motivate an unmotivated person? —How would you work with a difficult leader who has no vision? This book is a thorough, insightful response to those readers and anyone who feels they have plateaued on their journey to develop their ultimate potential. Every leader has room to grow, and the advice in these pages will help readers assess their current position, and structure an effective plan to achieve their goals." —Provided by publisher.
   Includes bibliographical references and index.
   ISBN 978-1-4555-4807-1 (hardback) — ISBN 978-1-4789-2432-6 (audiobook) — ISBN 978-1-4555-4805-7 (ebook) — ISBN 978-1-4555-4806-4 (Spanish ebook) — ISBN 978-1-4555-4803-3 (Spanish trade paperback) — ISBN 978-1-4789-2431-9 (audio download)   1. Leadership.   I. Title.
   HD57.7.M394256 2014
   658.4'092—dc23

                                                                                    2014008091

This book is dedicated to Collin Sewell. Every month for two years I answered a great question you sent me. As I mentored you from afar, I watched you grow from a good to a great leader. Now I enjoy mentoring you personally and am delighted to count you as a friend.

Contents

Acknowledgments

Thank you to:
Charlie Wetzel, my writer;
Stephanie Wetzel, for editing the early manuscript and
managing my social media;
Audrey Moralez, for her research assistance;
Carolyn Kokinda, for typing the first draft; and
Linda Eggers, my executive assistant.

PART I

Questions I Ask

1

Why Are Questions So Important?

Questions—for forty years I've asked questions on the subject of leadership. You might think that as time has gone by, and I've received thousands of answers, questions have become less important to me. But the opposite has been true. The more questions I ask, the more valuable I recognize them to be. Without the wise counsel and insightful answers I've received to questions over those decades, I wonder where I would be today. Certainly I would not have grown as much or come as far. The people who cared enough for me to give me guidance and advice when I asked questions have made a world of difference in my leadership.

Now that I'm in the second half of my life, people are asking me questions more and more. I think it's because they have come to see me as a father figure in the field of leadership. That's partly due to my age. But it's also because people sense my desire to add value to them and those who are hungry to learn often seek me out.

When I first began teaching leadership, I spent nearly all my time giving lectures. Today, at almost every speaking gig, people want time to ask me questions about leadership, which I welcome. Not only do I enjoy sharing what I've learned, but answering questions also gives me an opportunity to speak from my heart. As people share their issues and concerns with vulnerability, I try to share my experiences with transparency. I always want to help people who want to make a difference.

I've come to enjoy and value this experience so much that I wanted to write this book. It's my desire to show the impact that questions have made on my life, share the leadership questions I ask myself and others, and answer questions from people from many countries, backgrounds, and professions.

The Value of Questions

If you want to be successful and reach your leadership potential, you need to embrace asking questions as a lifestyle. Here's why:

1. You Only Get Answers to the Questions You Ask

Have you ever failed to ask a question because you thought it might be dumb? I have! Too many times I've allowed my desire not to look foolish to keep me from gaining knowledge that I needed. Richard Thalheimer, the founder of the Sharper Image, once asserted, "It is better to look uninformed than to be uninformed." For that reason we need to curb our egos and ask questions, even at the risk of looking foolish.

If you're worried that asking questions will make you look bad, let me give you some perspective. I enjoy reading Marilyn vos Savant's column in Sunday's *Parade* magazine. Listed in *Guinness World Records* for "Highest IQ," she answers difficult and often bewildering questions from readers. In her column of July 29, 2007, she decided to share questions she found difficult to answer, not because they were too tough, but because—well, take a look:

- "I notice you have the same first name as Marilyn Monroe. Are you related?"
- "Do you think daylight saving time could be contributing to global warming? The longer we have sunlight, the more it heats the atmosphere."
- "I see falling stars nearly every night. They seem to come out of nowhere. Have stars ever fallen out of any known constellations?"
- "When I dream, why don't I need my glasses to see?"
- "Can a ventriloquist converse with his dentist while his teeth are being worked on?"
- "I just observed a flock of geese flying in a 'V' formation. Is that the only letter they know?"[1]

Now don't you feel better about the quality of your questions?

If you want answers, you must ask questions. No one has helped me understand the value of questions more than my friend Bobb Biehl. In his book *Asking Profound Questions*, Bobb writes:

There is a gigantic difference between the person who has no questions to help him/her process situations and the person who has profound questions available. Here are a few of the differences:

WITHOUT PROFOUND QUESTIONS	WITH PROFOUND QUESTIONS
Shallow answers	Profound answers
Lack of confidence	Life confidence
Poor decision making	Wise decision making
Live in mental fog	Crystal clear focus in life
Work on low priorities	Focused on high priorities
Immature processing	Mature processing[2]

"The ability to ask the right question is more than half the battle of finding the answer."

—*Thomas J. Watson*

Asking the right question of the right person at the right time is a powerful combination because the answers you receive set you up for success. IBM founder Thomas J. Watson said, "The ability to ask the right question is more than half the battle of finding the answer." But that's true only if you are willing to ask the question.

2. Questions Unlock and Open Doors That Otherwise Remain Closed

Growing up I used to watch *Let's Make a Deal*, the TV show where contestants often got to choose among three doors to try to win the grand prize. It was fun to watch, but it was pure luck. Sometimes people won great stuff. Other times they got nothing.

In life's journey we face many doors. Hidden behind them are all kinds of possibilities leading to opportunities, experiences, and people, but the doors must be opened before we can go through them. Questions are the keys to opening these doors. For example, recently I had the privilege to interview former secretary of state Condoleezza Rice at Stanford University for the Leadercast event. Knowing that more than 150,000 people would be watching, I wanted to ask good questions of this amazing woman who has such extraordinary knowledge and life experiences so that we could learn from her. I spent days doing research, reading her books, and talking to people who would give me insight into her.

When I finally met her, I found her to be delightful and insightful. With each question I was able to open more doors of understanding into her experiences. By the end of our time I had found a wonderful friend. I learned a great deal, and I believe the rest of the audience did too.

Problem Solving Questions

As a leader you must always be looking forward for the sake of your team. When you face a problem and don't know what steps need to be taken to advance the team, ask the following questions:

- Why do we have this problem?
- How do we solve this problem?
- What specific steps must we take to solve this problem?

Management expert Peter Drucker said, "My greatest strength as a consultant is to be ignorant and ask a few questions." He knew the secret. Successful leaders relentlessly ask questions and have an incurable desire to pick the brains of the people they meet.

3. Questions Are the Most Effective Means of Connecting with People

I often watch speakers stand before an audience and work to build a case for their ideas. They would be more successful if instead they tried building a relationship with the people in the room. The word *communication* comes from the Latin word *communis*, meaning "common." Before we can communicate we must establish commonality. The greater the commonality, the greater the potential for connection and communication. The goal of effective communication is to prompt people to think, *Me too!* Too many speakers seem to elicit the thought *So what?*

The most effective way to connect with others is by asking questions. All of us have experienced the interest of others when we were lost and asked for directions. People will usually stop what they're doing to help others. Questions connect people.

Of course, you have to ask the right questions. In 2013 I was invited to play in the AT&T Pebble Beach National Pro-Am. Every golfer dreams of playing this great course, but being asked to play it with the best golfers in the world was beyond my dreams! For the event, another amateur and I were paired with two pros: Steve LeBrun and Aaron Watkins. We had such a great time. But let me tell you something: over the four days of golf with them, the professional golfers never once asked me any questions about golf. Not once did they ask me to help them line up a putt or to give advice about what club they should use. Why? Those weren't the right questions to ask me. I have nothing of value to offer them in that area of their lives. I am an amateur. On the other hand, they did ask me a lot of questions about personal growth, leadership, and book writing. In fact, they even asked if I would sign books for them.

What you ask matters. So does *how* you ask. If we want to connect with people, we can be like the census taker who had driven many miles down a remote country road to reach a mountain cabin. As he pulled up, a woman sitting on the porch yelled at him, "We don't want any. We're not buying anything."

"I'm not selling anything," the census taker said. "I'm here to take the census."

"We don't have one," the woman said.

"You don't understand," the census taker said. "We're trying to find out how many people there are in the United States."

"Well," she said, "you sure wasted your time driving out here to ask me, because I don't have any idea."

As playwright George Bernard Shaw observed, "The greatest problem with communication is the illusion that it has been accomplished."

> "The greatest problem with communication is the illusion that it has been accomplished."
> —*George Bernard Shaw*

4. Questions Cultivate Humility

Early in my career I didn't ask many questions. I mistakenly believed that as a leader I should know the answers to the people's questions. As a result, I adopted the ridiculous attitude of "fake it 'til you make it." Unfortunately, that caused me to do a lot of faking but very little making. It took time for me to become mature enough to say, "I don't know" and "I need your help."

Had I been wiser, I would have paid attention to the words of King Solomon, the wisest man who ever lived, who looked at the enormity of his leadership responsibilities and said, "I am only a little child and do not know how to carry out my duties."[3]

Paul Martinelli, the president of the John Maxwell Team, once told me, "All fear stems from either 'I am not enough' or 'I don't have enough.'" That's a keen insight. Too often, fear keeps us from being vulnerable and feeling secure enough to ask questions. When I was a young leader, I didn't feel wise enough, strong enough, mature enough, competent enough, confident enough, or qualified enough. When I began to be honest with myself, allow my weaknesses to humble me, and go to God for help, I began to change. I became more open and authentic. I was willing to admit my mistakes and weaknesses. I developed appropriate humility, and I began to change and grow.

My journey at that time was difficult and often lonely. I had to drop many bad habits. I had to change wrong priorities. I had to embrace new ways of thinking. I had to ask myself hard questions. Before, I had been unwilling to be wrong, and as a result I had been unable to discover what was right. Isn't it strange how we must surrender being right in order to find what's right, how humility enables us to be authentic, vulnerable, trustworthy, and intimate with others? People are open to those who are open to them.

5. Questions Help You to Engage Others in Conversation

Larry King, who has made his living speaking to people as a television talk show host, believes that asking questions is the secret of good conversation. He says,

I'm curious about everything, and if I'm at a cocktail party, I often ask my favorite question: "Why?" If a man tells me he and his family are moving to another city: "Why?" A woman is changing jobs: "Why?" Someone roots for the Mets: "Why?"

On my television show, I probably use this word more than any other. It's the greatest question ever asked, and it always will be. And it is certainly the surest way of keeping a conversation lively and interesting.[4]

Whenever I am preparing for a meeting with someone, I spend time determining what questions I want to ask. I do this because I want to make the most of the time I have, but I also do it to engage with the other person. I want people to know that I value them, and that, if possible, I want to add value to them. To do that, I believe I must get to know them. That requires that I ask questions, they talk, and I listen. And if I hope to receive value from people, again I need to ask questions and listen. You can't do these things unless you get to know people.

I encourage the use of questions to engage others and to learn from them. I believe you will find it one of the most rewarding practices you ever develop.

6. Questions Allow Us to Build Better Ideas

I am a strong believer in the power of ideas and of shared thinking. Any idea gets better when the right people get a chance to add to it and improve it. And good ideas can become great ones when people work together to improve them. I believe so strongly in this idea that in my book *How Successful People Think* I wrote a chapter called "Benefit from Shared Thinking."

Questions to Ask During a Learning Session

The meetings I look forward to most are the learning lunches I schedule every month with people who can teach me. When we meet, I come armed with questions. Many are specific to the individuals I'm meeting with. But there are some questions I try to ask everyone. You may want to use them too:

What is the greatest lesson you have learned? By asking this question I seek their wisdom.

What are you learning now? This question allows me to benefit from their passion.

How has failure shaped your life? This question gives insight into their attitude.

Who do you know whom I should know? This allows me to engage with their network.

What have you read that I should read? This question directs my personal growth.

What have you done that I should do? This helps me seek new experiences.

How can I add value to you? This shows my gratitude and desire to add value to them.

What is the key to shared thinking? Asking the right people the right questions. There's great power in doing that. As speaker Brian Tracy says, "A major stimulant to creative thinking is focused questions. There is something about a well-worded question that often penetrates to the heart of the matter and triggers new ideas and insights."

> "A major stimulant to creative thinking is focused questions."
> —*Brian Tracy*

In my early years of pastoring I attended an idea exchange led by very successful pastors. The genius of this event was that successful leaders shared their best practices with others who had the chance to ask questions. Young up-and-coming pastors also got to share their fresh ideas with more experienced leaders, who gave them feedback. The atmosphere of the conference was that of contagious hope and creative thinking because the entire experience was based on questions. It was a place where ideas were being reshaped into even better ideas.

I never forgot that experience, and later it was the catalyst for a monthly mentoring group called the Table, in which hand-selected leaders talk with me. The group met recently at a huge one-of-a-kind round table at the Arthur M. Blank Family Foundation in Atlanta. It was a magical day with great people asking great questions and adding value to each other. Because the Table members are from all over North America, most months we meet by phone. The interaction is fantastic as we discuss tough leadership issues and sharpen one another.

Whom to Invite to Your Table

As you bring people to your table to share ideas, be selective about whom you pick. Choose people who

- Understand the value of questions
- Desire the success of others
- Add value to others' thoughts
- Are not threatened by others' strengths
- Can emotionally handle quick changes in the conversation
- Understand their place of value at the table
- Bring out the best thinking in the people around them
- Have experienced success in the area under discussion
- Leave the table with a "we" attitude, not a "me" attitude

Any leader who asks the right questions of the right people has the potential to discover and develop great ideas. Inventor Thomas Edison observed, "The ideas I use are mostly the ideas of people who don't develop them." Making

> Any leader who asks the right questions of the right people has the potential to discover and develop great ideas.

it a practice to ask the right people the right questions will allow you to develop ideas to a whole new level.

7. Questions Give Us a Different Perspective

Too often, as leaders, we get fixated on our own point of view and spend our time trying to convince others of our opinions instead of trying to find out theirs. As English novelist and politician Edward George Earle Lytton Bulwer-Lytton asserted, "The true spirit of conversation consists in building on another man's observation, not overturning it."

That's where questions come into play. By asking questions and listening carefully to answers, we can discover valuable perspectives other than our own. That's valuable because we often make faulty assumptions about other people:

We believe people are good at the same things we are good at—they aren't.

We believe people are energized by the same things that energize us—they aren't.

We believe people see the big picture in the same way we do—they don't.

A wise leader once told me, "Before you attempt to *set* things right, make sure you *see* things right." That advice helped me to understand that most miscommunication is a result of people's having different assumptions. We can correct those wrong assumptions and prevent miscommunication by asking questions.

When I was the lead pastor at Skyline in San Diego, our staff did extensive interviews with people when they became members of the church. One of the questions we always asked was "What is the main thing you would change about the church?" That question paid great dividends because their fresh eyes saw things that ours did not. I would estimate that 80 percent of the positive changes we made were the result of what people told us in answer to those questions.

8. Questions Challenge Mind-Sets and Get You Out of Ruts

Too many people have flat-lined mentally. They've become stagnant. How do you fight against that? By asking the same question my friend Bill used to ask me: "When was the last time you had a good thought for the first time?"

Asking questions is a great way of preventing mental laziness and moving ourselves out of ruts. If you begin a task with certainties, you will probably end in doubts. But if you are willing to begin with doubts, you will likely end in certainties. Perhaps that's why someone once said, "The future belongs to the curious. The ones who are not afraid to try it, explore it, poke at it, question it, and turn it inside out."

> The future belongs to the curious.

Leadership author and trainer Mark Miller was listening to the 2012 TED presentations when he noticed that most had a trait in common: the talks had been prompted by a question beginning with *why*.

- "Why do children with rare diseases have to suffer?"—Jimmy Lin, a computer geneticist
- "Why can't we look for ancient archaeological sites from satellites?"—Sarah Parck, archaeologist

- "Why don't young people want to study neuroscience?"—Greg Gage, neuroscientist

If you want to make discoveries, if you want to disrupt the status quo, if you want to make progress and find new ways of thinking and doing, you need to ask questions. Questions are the first link in the chain of discovery and innovation.

Life-Changing

Speaker Anthony Robbins observed, "Quality questions create a quality life. Successful people ask bet-ter questions, and as a result, they get better answers." I have found that to be true. In fact, I don't think it would be an overstatement for me to say that questions have changed my life and become the markers of significant events.

> "Quality questions create a quality life. Successful people ask better questions, and as a result, they get better answers."
> —Anthony Robbins

Life is a journey, one in which we seek to find our way and make a difference. Questions help us to make that journey. In fact, the word *question* is derived from the Latin root word *quaerere* meaning "ask" or "seek." It has the same root as the word *quest*.[5] Sometimes the ques-tions come from others. Sometimes the questions are ones we ask. Either way, the answers mark us.

Life-Changing Questions Others Asked Me

Many wise and generous people have asked me questions that have positively affected my life. Though I could list hundreds or maybe thousands of questions others have asked that helped me, I want to share with you the top ten:

1. "What do you want to do with your life?" —Dad

More than any other person on earth, my father influenced me. He guided my early journey with wisdom and strength. He not only asked me this question, he also helped me find the answer. He suggested that I had good people skills and that my life should include connecting with and helping others. All my life I have tried to add value to people because he asked me this question.

2. "Do you know you're a leader?" —Mr. Horton

I've been influenced by many teachers. Mr. Horton taught me in fifth grade. When I was elected to be the "judge" by my classmates and he saw that I was always choosing the teams at recess, he recognized my leadership behavior. He understood that leadership was influence. He not only observed my leadership behavior but pointed it out to me and started me out on my leadership journey.

3. "Do you have a plan for your personal growth?" —Curt Kampmeier

How would I have known that a breakfast meeting with a seminar trainer would be the beginning of my lifelong personal growth journey? Curt's question caused me to search myself and find myself wanting. It was the catalyst for my growth. And because I know the power of that question, I have asked it in hundreds of conferences of tens of thousands of people. Today, many successful people can point to that question as the beginning of their growth journey too.

4. "Can I help you get started in business?" —Tom Phillippe

I started my career in the ministry, but I've always had an innovative mind-set, a kind of entrepreneurial spirit. Tom is a lifelong friend who wanted to help me grow financially and gave me an opportunity to invest in my future. I borrowed the money I needed for the investment and Tom made sure it was secure and successful. Truly, I think money is overrated in our culture, but it does give a person options, and for that I am grateful. Tom's question and my willingness to respond brought about an amazing benefit to my life.

5. *"How can we receive regular ongoing training from you?"*
—Thirty-one attendees of a leadership conference

After I spent a day teaching leadership at a Holiday Inn in Jackson, Mississippi, one of the conference attendees asked me that question, and others chimed in. They wanted to receive ongoing leadership training after the conference. After giving it some quick thought I said, "What if I recorded a monthly leadership lesson and sent it to you for five dollars a month?" All thirty-one people signed up and gave me their contact information, and I went home and figured out what to do. I taught a leadership lesson to my staff, recorded it, and mailed out tapes to subscribers. That was the beginning of what is now the Maximum Impact Club. That subscription list quickly grew to more than ten thousand people and has continued to train leaders for the last thirty years. It also was the start of my developing training resources, and of what would eventually become The John Maxwell Company.

6. *"What could we do to make a difference?" —Larry Maxwell*

My brother has been a major influence in my life from the time we were kids. No one challenges me more than he does. He asked me this question in 1995, and it became the catalyst for the founding of EQUIP, the largest leadership training organization in the world. Millions of trained leaders in more than 175 countries have benefited because Larry asked that question.

7. *"What will you do with the second half of your life?" —Bob Buford*

Bob is a friend, but I was confronted with this question when I read his book *Half Time*. Here is the passage that grabbed my attention:

You will not get very far in your second half without knowing your life mission. Can yours be stated in a sentence or two?
A good way to begin formulating one is with some questions
(and nakedly honest answers). What is your passion? What
have you achieved? What have you done uncommonly well?
How are you wired? Where do you belong? What are the
"shoulds" that have trailed you during the first half? These and
other questions like them will direct you toward the self your
heart longs for; they will help you discover the task for which
you were especially made.

For the last twenty years, thanks to Bob's question, my efforts have
been focused on adding value to leaders who multiply value to others.

8. "Will you call me anytime you need help?" —John Bright Cage

John is a cardiologist who slipped me his card in 1998 over lunch.
He wrote his cell number on it, telling me that I wasn't healthy and
was a candidate for a heart attack. Six months later, at our company
Christmas party, I suffered the heart attack he had warned me about.
A call to him by my assistant Linda Eggers in the middle of the night
led to a series of actions that saved my life. I credit the things I've
accomplished during the fifteen years since to the efforts of him and
the rest of the medical team.

9. "Would you like to start a coaching company?" —Paul Martinelli and Scott M. Fay

I was sixty-three years old and wrapping up a successful career
when Scott and Paul approached me, saying they had a great idea: the
three of us should start a coaching company. I didn't need or want
another responsibility, so I initially said no. Thankfully, they were persistent and wouldn't stop asking the question. After many conversations over an eighteen-month period, I finally said yes. Today I am

grateful for the question and their persistence because the thousands of John Maxwell Team coaches who have been trained and released around the world are a continual source of joy to me. We are experiencing life-changing memories together.

10. "Will you trust me with your life?" —God

I know that you may not be a person of faith, so this question may not make sense to you. But I would be remiss if I didn't share it with you. As a young man of seventeen, I gave my life to God. That was the greatest decision of my life! I agree with Ralph Waldo Emerson, who wrote, "All I have seen teaches me to trust the Creator for all I have not seen." The longer I live the more I trust Him. By the way, when God asks you a question, it's not for His benefit. It's for yours.

Questions I Asked That Changed My Life

Those key questions asked by others have certainly marked me. However, just as impacting have been some key questions I have asked of others, beginning when I was a child. Here are the ten questions—and answers—that have made the greatest impact on my life:

1. "Mom, how much do you love me?"

As a child I asked my mother this question repeatedly. It wasn't because I doubted the answer; it was because I reveled in it. Mom's answer was always the same: "With all my heart, unconditionally." And often she would go on to explain that her unconditional love meant that she would always love me no matter what I did.

Mom used to tell me that I could always talk to her and she would always listen and understand. And it was true. She lived those words not only when I was a child, but as I grew into adulthood. For sixty-three years I lived within the security of my mother's love. She knew me well and loved me in spite of myself. When she passed away, she left an empty place in my heart that can never be filled by another person. I credit much of my success and willingness to take risks to the unconditional love she always gave me.

2. "Margaret, will you marry me?"

One summer at youth camp I was dating a girl named Marsha. When she introduced me to a friend named Margaret, I was stunned. The moment I saw Margaret, I said to myself, "I'm holding the wrong girl's hand." I immediately began pursuing Margaret. We dated in high school and college, and after the greatest sales job in the history of mankind, she married me.

Margaret is the love of my life and my most trusted advisor. She has been a vital part of every decision we have made for over forty years of marriage. In our early years, she helped carry a heavy workload and released me to pursue my calling with full-on commitment. Today my greatest joy is spending time with her.

3. "Pastor, how did you build a great church?"

As a young pastor I was influenced by the books of Elmer Towns, who wrote much about church growth. He highlighted America's great churches and the pastors who led them, which created a hunger in me to grow a large church.

Inspired by the stories I read about the top ten churches in the country, I began to call their leaders and ask each for an appointment so I could ask questions. Since they didn't know me and I wanted to make it worth their while, I offered a hundred dollars for thirty minutes of their time (which was about a week's worth of my annual salary). A few said yes.

For the next four years I visited the churches of the leaders who agreed to meet with me, and I asked them questions about their success. When I finished this project I came to this conclusion: "Everything rises and falls on leadership." That truth has been the centerpiece of my leadership journey, and has prompted me to teach others to lead for the rest of my life.

4. "Les, why do you write books?"

It was never my intention to be an author. I loved reading books, but never had a desire to write—that is, until I asked my author friend Les Parrott why he wrote. His answer changed my life. He said, "I write books to influence people I will never meet. Books increase my audience and my message."

The moment I heard that, I decided I needed to write. The idea of making an impact on people I would never meet fueled the passion I already possessed for what I taught. Where I had not possessed a desire for writing, my desire to influence more people made me want to write. Today, twenty-five million books later, my dream has been realized.

5. "Dad, can I have your blessing to leave this organization?"

This was the hardest question I ever asked. Why? My father was a leader of the organization I wanted to leave, and he had spent his entire life investing in the people in it. I had grown up in it and it was all I knew. My friends were there. My history was there. It was safe.

But I also understood that my future could not be there. If I wanted to keep growing and pursue what I believed to be my calling, I knew I would have to chart new territory. I would have to leave all I knew to learn what I didn't know. With tears, my father gave me his blessing.

That question—and his gracious, unselfish answer—unlocked the door and allowed me to walk toward an unlimited future.

6. "Leaders, what am I required to do that no one else can do except me?"

The interview had been long and I had answered dozens of questions asked by the leaders of Skyline Church's search committee. They were inviting me to become the leader of the most influential Wesleyan church in the world. It was a great privilege. I would be following Orval Butcher, the founding pastor who had led them for twenty-seven years. He had done everything for the church and was greatly revered and loved. But I also knew it would be a great challenge. I knew I would not be able to fill his shoes or the search committee's expectations.

When they finished asking every question they had, I asked mine. I wanted to know the responsibilities that only I could assume. That question led to a two-hour conversation and provided a foundation upon which I could lead.

I gave the congregation fourteen years of my life, and Skyline was named one of the ten most influential churches in America while I was there. It was a fantastic privilege to serve there and one of the best experiences of my life.

7. "Charlie, will you help me write books?"

Learning to write was no easy task for me. While writing my first book, I worked for four hours one night in a hotel room and had only one poorly written paragraph to show for it. But I persevered. And after many months of effort I completed *Think on These Things*. It contained thirty-three chapters, each of which was only three to four pages, but it was a start.

Over the next fourteen years, I authored a total of nine books, but I desired to do more. That's when I asked Charlie Wetzel to help me. We started writing together in 1994. In the twenty years since, we've written over sixty-five books together and sold more than 24 million copies. Of all my inner circle, he has affected more people than anyone else.

8. "Kevin, can I mentor you?"

In 1995 I decided that I wanted to mentor ten people on an ongoing basis. I did that because I knew that adding value to people with high potential who are hungry to grow is one of the best investments a leader can make. I've continued to do that every year since.

Over the years, the list of people I'm mentoring has continued to change, but I have always handpicked the people I invest in. No one has given a greater return on the time I am investing than Kevin Myers. The church he founded, 12Stone, is now one of the fastest-growing and most influential congregations in America. I have watched him blossom from a good leader to a fantastic one.

A few years ago he told me that he intended to build a leadership center that would train leaders from around the world, and he asked if he could name it after me. I was astounded by the request. It had once been a vision of mine to do what he was doing, and this felt like a fulfillment of a lost dream.

"I would be honored," I answered. "What would my obligations be?"

"Just use this facility to inspire and train leaders," Kevin replied. "That's all."

Kevin's answer blew me away. Today the John Maxwell Leadership Center is strategically located near Atlanta, Georgia, and is training leaders around the world. I believe it will establish a leadership legacy that will outlive me. And it all began because I asked a question of a young pastor with unlimited potential.

9. "Jeff, whom do you know that I should know?"

Many years ago I started making it a practice to ask this question whenever I met someone for the first time. Occasionally it has produced no results. Often it leads to my meeting someone helpful or interesting. But when I asked Jeff Brown this question, it changed my life. Why? Because Jeff introduced me to John Wooden, one of the greatest coaches and teachers of our time.

Often I talk about Coach Wooden and the guidance and wisdom he imparted to my life. After Jeff's introduction, Coach Wooden and I became friends and he became my mentor. He taught me more than any other person and inspired me to write my books *Today Matters* and *Sometimes You Win—Sometimes You Learn.*

I want to encourage you. When you meet interesting people, the odds are high that they know others who are interesting. The old saying is true: birds of a feather flock together. Ask the question and I believe it will open the door to some wonderful new friends and interesting opportunities.

10. "Reader, how can I add value to you?"

Years ago I was challenged by another author, who said, "As I write I always ask the question, 'Will the reader turn the page?' " I started asking that same question as I began to write books. I believe the answer will be yes as long as on each page I am able to add value to you. That is certainly my desire for this book. Adding value is more than just words to me. It's a concept that defines my life. And as long as I can ask that question and believe the answer will be yes, I will continue writing books to try to help you and other potential readers.

Statesman-philanthropist Bernard Baruch said, "Millions saw the apple fall, but Newton was the only one who asked why." Because Newton took the time to ask questions, the world benefited from his theory of gravity.

> "Millions saw the apple fall, but Newton was the only one who asked why."
> —*Bernard Baruch*

Questions have power. When I look back at the progression of my life, I can see that questions have marked the way for my growth, prompted positive changes of direction, and led to many successes. Though many of us try to make ourselves look smart by giving clever answers, we would be much better off if we focused our attention on asking questions. If we ask good questions of the right people, we will have a wonderful return for our lives. Never forget: good questions inform; great questions transform!

> Good questions inform; great questions transform.

What questions have others asked of you that have made a positive difference in your life? What questions have you asked others that are helping you even today? Become intentional from this point on in being a questioner. You should even ask questions of yourself. I do. In fact, that is the focus of the next chapter.

2

What Questions Do I Ask Myself as a Leader?

As a young leader starting out in my career, I was always in a hurry. Filled with passion and vision, I had an urgent agenda to pursue, which prompted me to try to get buy-in from others. I gave a lot of directions and asked very few questions because of this. As a result, I was often wrong but seldom in doubt.

My attitude changed when I made a wrong decision that affected several people in my organization. That's when I realized that when a leader makes a bad decision, it affects not only him but many other people. That gave me pause. While personal maturity may mean being able to see *beyond* yourself, leadership maturity means considering others *before* yourself. I recognized that I could no longer be a Lone Ranger, doing my own thing and asking others to do my bidding. I needed to think ahead and consider others.

> While personal maturity may mean being able to see *beyond* yourself, leadership maturity means considering others *before* yourself.

I started doing that by asking questions. I explained in chapter one how important questions are. Questions are the basis of learning. But they are also a foundation for better leadership. I realized that during a conversation with one of my mentors, Coach John Wooden, former basketball coach of the UCLA Bruins. We were having lunch. As usual for these sessions, I had prepared for hours and had a list of questions on a legal pad. What he said wasn't even in response to one of my questions. He simply mentioned it in passing, but it grabbed my attention. Coach said, "John, there is one question I ask myself every day."

My heart leaped with anticipation as I waited to hear an insight from this highly successful coach known for great wisdom. I'll share with you what the actual question was later in this chapter. While it has value, the practice he was sharing was even more valuable. I realized in that moment that good leaders ask *themselves* questions.

After my session with Coach, I couldn't wait to get home, spend some time in my thinking chair, and write down what questions I should be asking myself every day as a leader. The questions I discovered are what I'm going to share with you in this chapter.

What You Need to Ask Yourself

If you are a leader, you understand that questions are always a part of a leader's life. The issue becomes, who is asking the questions? As a leader, I can allow others to ask me the hard and important questions, or I can take responsibility, be proactive, and ask those questions of myself. I have come to the realization that by asking myself tough questions, I can maintain my integrity, increase my energy, and improve my leadership capacity.

Since writing out the questions I ask myself as a leader, I've reviewed and reflected on them hundreds of times. Many of these questions are personal, but I believe they can also help you as much as they have me. I pass them on to you as a guide, with the suggestion that you develop your own list.

1. Am I Investing in Myself? A Question of Personal Growth

The most important investment you and I will ever make is in ourselves. That investment will determine the return that we get out of life. Jim Rohn's mentor John Earl Shoaff said to him, "Jim, if you want to be wealthy and happy, learn this lesson well: learn to work harder on yourself than you do on your job." Jim did learn that lesson well. As he once pointed out, "The book you don't read can't help you; the seminar you won't attend can't change your life. The business gets better when you get better. Never wish it were easier, wish you were better."

Since 1974 I have been intentionally investing in myself, and for nearly as long I have been encouraging others to do likewise. Some people do; others don't. Why is that? I believe three main factors come into play. These will determine if or how you will invest in yourself:

Your Self-Image: How You See Yourself

How do you feel about yourself as a person? Are you positive? Are you negative? On a scale of 1 to 10, what number would you use to describe how you feel about yourself? Take a moment and rate yourself.

Whatever number you picked to describe your self-image also describes your willingness to invest in yourself. For example, if you rated your self-image at a 5, you will be willing to invest in yourself up to a 5 level, but not more. That's why people with low self-images do not make great investments in themselves. It's not what you are that keeps you from investing in yourself; it's what you think you are—or are not. You will never be able to bet on yourself unless you believe in yourself.

> You will never be able to bet on yourself unless you believe in yourself.

Many people find themselves thinking like Snoopy, the beagle in the *Peanuts* comic strip who thinks, "Yesterday I was a dog. Today I'm a dog. Tomorrow I'll probably still be a dog. Sigh.

There's so little hope for advancement!" To do that is to sell themselves short. People are not stuck in dead-end situations when it comes to their potential. We have the ability to make tremendous advances. But first we must believe in ourselves.

Your Dream: How You See Your Future

When I sat down to write *Put Your Dream to the Test*, my desire was to help people make great strides toward their dreams. What I didn't realize until the book had been written and I starting speaking about it was that many people don't have a dream. I was shocked. My life has been filled with hopes, dreams, and aspirations. Because of that, I assumed that everyone had at least one dream. I was wrong. Why does that matter? Because the size of your dream determines the size of your investment. If your dream is large, you will invest in yourself to achieve it. If you have no dream, you may not invest in yourself at all.

My start in leadership was very unimpressive. I led an old country church attended by a few farmers. But my passion to help people was huge. It filled me with energy. My dream was to build a great church.

We made very little money in those days. I was paid eighty dollars a week and Margaret worked half days as a kindergarten teacher. We barely scraped by. But because I had big dreams, I was always looking for ways to improve myself and my leadership. Any time I went to a bookstore it felt like Christmas. I'd come home loaded with books to help me grow. And I was always on the lookout for conferences that would help me. Margaret would cringe because it put such a strain on our budget, but she always made it work. She believed in me as much as I believed in myself. The dreams we shared for our future were bigger than our surroundings or circumstances, and fueled our desire to grow.

Your Friends: How Others See You

Motivational speaker Joe Larson once said, "My friends didn't believe I could become a successful speaker, so I did something about it. I went out and found some new friends." That may sound harsh, but that is what's needed for anyone who is surrounded by people who don't believe in them.

One of my most important growth decisions was to expand my horizons and find other people whose passion to grow themselves and help others was similar to mine. At that time I was only thirty-three years old, and I left everything familiar and everyone I knew. That decision took courage. However, if I had stayed where I was, I would never have grown to the next level.

People need others to help them stay inspired and growing. Missionary doctor Albert Schweitzer asserted, "In everyone's life, at some time, our inner fire goes out. It is then burst into flame by an encounter with another human being. We should all be thankful for those people who rekindle the inner spirit." If you have friends who light your inner fire, you are very fortunate; they will make you want to keep investing in yourself and growing. If you don't, find some, because nothing is more important for your potential as a leader than your personal daily growth.

2. Am I Genuinely Interested in Others?
A Question of Motivation

Someone once said, "People have two reasons for doing anything— a good reason and the real reason." For you to be a good leader when dealing with people, the good reason must be the same as the real reason. Your motives matter.

If you are a leader—or want to become one—you need to ask yourself why. There is a big difference between people who want to lead because they are genuinely interested in others and desire to help them, and people who are in it to help only themselves. People who lead for selfish reasons seek...

- **Power:** They love control and will continue to add value to themselves by reducing the value of others.
- **Position:** Titles are their ego food. They continually make sure that others feel their authority and know their rights as a leader.
- **Money:** They will use people and sell themselves for financial gain.
- **Prestige:** Their looking good is more important to them than their being and doing good.

It's easy for a leader to lose focus. That's why I need to check my motives daily. I never want to put my leadership ahead of the people I lead.

Naturally gifted leaders have capabilities that they can easily use for personal advantage. They see things before others do, and they often see more than others see. As a result, they enjoy the advantage of having good timing and seeing the big picture. That puts them in a position to make the most of opportunities.

If I can see something before you do, I can get started before you, and that often guarantees a win. If I see more than you see, my decisions will likely be better than yours. I win again! So the question is not "Does the leader have an advantage over others?" The answer to that question is yes. The question is "Will the leader use that advantage for personal gain or for the benefit of everyone on the team?" That is why I need to ask myself whether I am genuinely interested in others. It keeps my natural selfishness in check and purifies my motives.

Leaders are always in danger of abusing their power. That is why when I addressed leaders at the United Nations, I spoke on the subject "Three Questions People Ask of Their Leader." Those questions are:

Can you help me? That is a competence question.
Do you care for me? That is a compassion question.
Can I trust you? That is a character question.

Note that two of those questions deal with a leader's motives. If followers are concerned about the motivation of leaders, the leaders themselves should be too.

Let me say one more thing about this subject: questioning your motives is not the same as questioning your character. If you have poor character, your motives will probably be bad. But if you have solid character, you can still fall prey to bad motives. Motives are usually attached to specific situations or actions. Character is based on values. If you have wrong motives in a particular situation, but your values are good and your character is strong, you will probably detect where you're going wrong and have a chance to correct it.

This is the reason we've begun teaching values to leaders through my nonprofit organization, EQUIP. When leaders learn and live good values, they make themselves more valuable and lift the value of other people. That is the foundation of positive leadership.

> When leaders learn and live good values, they make themselves more valuable and lift the value of other people.

3. Am I Grounded as a Leader? A Question of Stability

Just as leaders are vulnerable to acting for their personal advantage, they are also susceptible to having an overblown sense of their own importance. That's why they need to remain grounded. What do I mean by that? Good leaders need to exhibit three important qualities:

Humility: Understanding Your Place in Light of the Bigger Picture

I once read that at the height of the Roman Empire, certain generals were honored with a *triumph*, a procession of honor through the city of Rome in which the general was preceded by marching legions, trumpeting heralds, and the enemies who had been conquered and captured in the victory. As the general rode in a chariot and was cheered by virtually everyone in the city, a slave held a laurel wreath above his head to signify his victory. But as the procession continued, the slave had one additional responsibility. He was to whisper the following words into the general's ear: "Hominem te memento," meaning, "Remember you are only a man."

Leaders can start to think that everything is all about them—especially when their team or organization is winning. The greater the accomplishment, the greater the need to check their egos. That's why it's so important that they remain grounded. The most important quality of a well-grounded person is humility.

What is humility? My friend Rick Warren says, "Humility is not denying your strengths. Humility is being honest about your weaknesses. All of us are a bundle of both great strengths and great weaknesses and humility is being able to be honest about both."[6] My belief is that humility is a choice every day to give credit to God for our blessings and to other people for our successes.

> "Humility is not denying your strengths. Humility is being honest about your weaknesses."
> —Rick Warren

Humble leaders are comfortable with who they are and feel no need to draw attention to themselves. They revel in the accomplishments of others, empower others to excel, and allow others to shine. That doesn't mean that a leader needs to blend into the woodwork. It just means having the right perspective. Leadership author Patrick Lencioni says that good leaders can motivate others and be humble at the same time. He writes, "I have defined humility as the realization that a leader is inherently no better than the people he or she leads, and charisma as the realization that the leader's actions are more important than those of the people he or she leads. As leaders, we must strive to embrace humility and charisma."

I recently read a story about a leader who exemplifies charismatic humility: Angela Ahrendts. For seven years she was the CEO of Burberry, a luxury fashion house headquartered in London. While leading the company, she transformed its brand, increased its global reputation, and more than tripled its annual sales and its value.

Ahrendts is known as an innovator, but she is also known for being the kind of leader who promotes collaboration, fosters team spirit, and builds trust. The key? Ahrendts says, "It's compassion. It's humility. It's saying thank you."[7]

At only fifty-three years old, Ahrendts was set at Burberry and could have continued there until she decided to retire. Instead she did something that surprised many people. She chose to step down as CEO at that company to become a senior vice-president of Apple. As writer Jeff Chu asked, "Why would a CEO become someone else's underling?"[8] Because a grounded leader who is humble is willing to take on a new challenge, even though it means taking risks, giving up power, and losing a degree of autonomy.

Authenticity: Being Comfortable in Your Own Skin

Successful leaders are often put on pedestals by people. To stay real and grounded, leaders need to get off that pedestal and stay with the people. They do that by being honest and authentic. Maybe that's why Mark Batterson, an author and the lead pastor of National Community Church in Washington, D.C., identifies authenticity as the new authority in leadership.

If you are a leader, your goal is to lift up your people, not have them lift you up. If you allow others to put you on a pedestal or if you minimize your faults and accentuate your successes, you create what I call the Success Gap. That's a perceived distance between successful people and those who are less successful. Inauthentic people enjoy that gap, protect their image, try to stay above the crowd, and, if anything, make the gap look even larger.

In contrast, authentic leaders work hard to close that gap. How? They are open about their failures and shortcomings. They use self-deprecating humor and laugh at themselves. When they are asked to speak, they prefer simple introductions, and they walk among the people and connect with them before and after their time onstage. They do everything they can to be themselves without pretense.

Calling: Having a Purpose That Is Bigger than You

The third thing that can keep leaders grounded is their calling. Recently during a Q and A session I was asked the difference between a dream and a calling. My answer was that a dream is something you really *want* to do, but a calling is something

> A dream is something you really *want* to do, but a calling is something you *have* to do.

you *have* to do. Look at the lives of people like Thomas Edison, Henry Ford, Mother Teresa, Martin Luther King Jr., and Steve Jobs. They were people who felt compelled to do their life's work.

Every day I wake up knowing that my calling is to add value to leaders so they can multiply value to others. This is what I've been doing for the last forty years. It's who I am. It's what I know. It's what I want and love to do. It's not work. As the old saying goes, work isn't work unless you'd rather be doing something else. I don't want to do anything else.

> Work isn't work unless you'd rather be doing something else.

Author and marketing expert Seth Godin advises, "Instead of wondering what your next vacation is, maybe you should set up a life you don't need to escape from." I think that's something everyone should aspire to. There's nothing like doing what you were created for. I know that for me . . .

When I found my why, I found my way.
When I found my why, I found my will.
When I found my why, I found my wings.

I never want to become a leader so full of himself that he becomes unable to fulfill his purpose. Leaders who do that become unstable. That's why I check myself to make sure that I remain grounded. If I maintain humility, display authenticity, and remain true to my calling, the chances are good that I'll be able to keep my feet on the ground.

4. Am I Adding Value to My Team? A Question of Teamwork

I shared with you at the beginning of the chapter that John Wooden said to me in one of our mentoring sessions, "There is one question I ask myself every day." Here's what he said: "Every day I ask myself, how can I make my team better?" Not only did that question inspire me to create my own list of questions to ask myself as a leader, but it's such a good question that it also made my list.

As a leader, I need to figure out what I can do to make my team better, to add value to the players and promote teamwork. Here are my suggestions for adding value, based on what I learned from Coach Wooden. Every day, I try to do the following:

Promote Full Commitment

Executive speaking coach Patricia Fripp says, "A team is a group of people who may not be equal in experience, talent, or education but in commitment." A team whose members aren't committed is doomed to perform unevenly when the heat is on. That commitment must start with the leader and extend to the entire team.

> "A team is a group of people who may not be equal in experience, talent, or education but in commitment."
> —Patricia Fripp

When Coach Wooden noticed that a player wasn't giving 100 percent in practice, he would take that person aside and say, "I know you think you can make up tomorrow for what you don't do today, but that is impossible. If you are giving 50 percent today, you can't give 150 percent tomorrow! You can never give more than 100 percent."

If you are a leader, the true measure of your success is not getting people to work. It's not getting people to work hard. It is getting people to work hard together. That takes commitment.

Create an Environment of Encouragement and Support

One of the nicest things about teamwork is that you always have others on your side. It's pulling together, not pulling apart. It's many voices, one heart. But that often doesn't occur unless there is an environment of encouragement and support. Leaders need to take responsibility for working to create that.

One of the ways Coach Wooden used to do that was to ask his players to acknowledge the skills and contributions of others. He told each player that if a teammate made a great pass or set a pick that allowed him to score, he should acknowledge the teammate on the way back down the court. One time a player asked, "Coach, if we do that, what if the teammate that made the assist isn't looking?" Coach Wooden replied, "He will always be looking." Coach knew that people look for and thrive on acknowledgment and appreciation.

Identify Adversity as an Opportunity to Develop Character

Teamwork is never tested during good times. You know how good your team is when adversity hits. It introduces you to yourself, and it reveals where you're strong and where you're weak. We often don't like that, but the reality is that losses can be learning experiences if your attitude is right. Author and apologist C. S. Lewis took that thought one step further. He wrote, "God allows us to experience the low points of life in order to teach us lessons we could not learn in any other way."

Coach Wooden told me that in the early years of his coaching, his team did not have a basketball arena of its own, so all of its games were played at the arenas of opponents. That sure seems as if it would be a hardship. However, Coach felt that this disadvantage to his team became an advantage during the NCAA tournament, because his team was used to playing on the road. We would be wise to look for the opportunity in adversity and learn from it.

Consider Each Person's Strengths and Weaknesses

One night I was having dinner with former college football coach Lou Holtz, friend and businessman Collin Sewell, and other friends in Odessa, Texas. As we sat and talked about leadership and teamwork, Lou said something that grabbed my attention: "The freedom to do your own thing ends when you have obligations and responsibilities. If you want to fail yourself you can—but you cannot do your own thing if you have responsibilities to team members."

> "The freedom to do your own thing ends when you have obligations and responsibilities."
> —Lou Holtz

I believe that's true. If you are a team leader, you must take responsibility for helping your team to succeed. A big part of that is knowing what everyone's strengths and weaknesses are and using everyone's strengths to help the team win. You can do that by asking, "What's best for the rest?"

Many people don't think to ask that question. Why? Because people are often naturally focused on themselves. Here's an example. When a group picture is taken with you in it, who is the first person you look for when you see the picture? Yourself. How do you determine if it's a good picture? It usually depends on how good you look in it. Only after you've checked your own image do you begin looking at everyone else's.

Teamwork demands that we focus a little less on ourselves and a little more on how the team looks. To succeed, we must value completing one another more highly than competing with one another. If we want the team to win, we can't be like the man in the comic strip who says to his friend, "There may not be an 'I' in team, but there is an 'M' and an 'E,' and that spells me!'"

Good leaders are like good coaches. They know how to bring out the best in the people on their team. That's what John Wooden did. It's also what legendary NFL coach Vince Lombardi did. When he took over the Green Bay Packers, the team had suffered through eleven straight losing seasons. Lombardi turned the team around in one season. How? By discovering the strengths and weaknesses of his players and helping them to perform at their best. In particular, Bart Starr, Jim Taylor, and Paul Hornung—all of whom had sat on the bench under Lombardi's predecessor—excelled. In fact all three of them ended up in the Hall of Fame.

If you are a leader and you are not adding value to your team, you need to question whether or not you should even *be* the leader. Adding value to team members and helping them to win are what leadership is all about.

5. Am I Staying in My Strength Zone? A Question of Effectiveness

Of all the questions I ask myself as a leader, this one has done the most to help me reach my potential. But I didn't know to ask it at the beginning of my career. In fact, when I started in leadership, I didn't even know I had a strength zone! I did everything. In addition, I spent too much time on the wrong things and mistook activity for progress.

Poet and critic Samuel Johnson wrote, "Almost every man wastes part of his life in attempts to display qualities he does not possess." That was me. But that's OK. In the beginning of our lives, we have to do many tasks that don't play to our strengths. In fact, if we don't do a lot of things,

> "Almost every man wastes part of his life in attempts to display qualities he does not possess."
> —*Samuel Johnson*

we won't be able to *find* our strengths. But it's sad if after several years in our careers we still haven't discovered our strengths. Solomon, the wisest man who ever lived, said, "A gift opens the way and ushers the giver into the presence of the great."[9] How can we ever reach our potential if we don't know what we do well?

I was fortunate to have parents who recognized, encouraged, and cultivated my strengths, so I got an early start in life in this area. But I also worked at learning about them. I tried new things. I asked people for constructive feedback. And I used tools to help me understand who I am. One that I often recommend to others is StrengthsFinder. Developed by members of the Gallup organization, it is a survey that nearly ten million people have used to discover their top five natural strengths.

As I discovered my strengths, I disciplined myself to work within and improve on those strengths. As I grew in them, I developed my uniqueness and found a greater sense of purpose. Philosopher-poet Ralph Waldo Emerson asserted, "Each man has his own vocation; his talent is his call. There is one direction in which all space is open to him." What he is describing is moving toward the unlimited potential each of us has when we find and stay in our strength zone.

Staying in your strengths gives you an advantage. In a world where people spend much of their time shoring up their weaknesses, your focus on maximizing your strengths will set you apart from others. That's good. However, your temptation as a leader may be to leverage that advantage selfishly for personal gain. As Daniel Vasella, chairman of Novartis AG, says, "When you achieve good results...you are typically celebrated, and you begin to believe that the figure at the center of all that champagne toasting is yourself." You must guard against that.

Staying in your strengths also gives you opportunities. You don't want to miss them. In the foreword of my friend Kevin Hall's book *Aspire*, Stephen R. Covey writes,

The root of opportunity is port, meaning the entryway by water into a city or place of business. In earlier days, when the tide and winds were right and the port opened, it allowed entry to do commerce, to visit, or to invade and conquer. But only those who recognized the opening could take advantage of the open port, or opportunity.[10]

The more you focus on your strengths, the better you will be positioned to see and seize opportunities as they arise.

If you haven't already done so, when you discover your talents, gifts, and strengths, you will come to a point of decision. Will you use them to coast along? Or will you dig into the hard work of developing them?

Someone who did this was Major League pitcher Nolan Ryan. There was no question that Ryan had talent. He pitched his first no-hitter before he was in high school. And as a high school pitcher, he once struck out twenty-one batters in a single game. It was said that he threw the ball so hard that he broke bones in the hands of his catchers. But when Ryan made it to the Major Leagues, he realized he could not simply rely on his talent. He had to improve it. Ryan explains,

> All I knew was to throw as hard as I could for as long as I could. Early in my career in the big leagues, when I would get in trouble I would resort back to that mindset. Finally, after being unsuccessful with that approach—I learned that when I was just throwing hard I was throwing wild and walking guys and losing games—it finally dawned on me. If I didn't make an adjustment or change, then I was going to be one of those players who was very gifted, but didn't make a lot out of it.... A lot of people get here with the God-given ability, the gift that they received. But to stay here and have a lengthy career takes a commitment to make sacrifices that most won't continually

make. Talent may get you here, but it takes work, real work, to stay here, and it takes development of the mental side of your game to separate yourself on this level.[11]

Ryan did separate himself, so much so that he ended up in the Hall of Fame. He played at the highest level until age forty-six. By the time he retired, he had won 324 games, recorded 5,714 strikeouts (the most in history), struck out 383 batters in one season (another record), and pitched seven no-hitters (also the most in history). That's what you call staying in your strength zone!

6. Am I Taking Care of Today? A Question of Success

Good leaders naturally look to the future. They are known for vision and for leading others to new and higher destinations. However, the future isn't where anything gets accomplished. That happens *today*. That's why you need to take care of it.

John Wooden would often say, "Make every day your masterpiece." How do we do that? By making each day count. We need to have the words of former Israeli prime minister Golda Meir ringing in our ears every day. She said, "I must govern the clock, not be governed by it."

> **"I must govern the clock, not be governed by it."**
> —*Golda Meir*

Getting your hands around what you should be doing every day can be difficult. To best use my time correctly, there are five areas where I want to make sure I'm taking care of business. I can't do everything every day, but I can do the most important things every day. Here is what's on my list:

Faith

Former president Jimmy Carter asserted, "My faith demands that I do whatever I can, wherever I am, whenever I can, for as long as I can with whatever I have to try to make a difference." That's a great perspective. Because I agree with that, I must be sure to exercise and live out my faith every day.

For me, faith means bringing God into the picture every day. And that's good news. Looking at everything with God in the picture gives me a sense of security and resilience. When your day is filled with those two qualities, you will have a good day.

Family

For many years now my definition of success has been having those who are closest to me love and respect me the most. Why? Because if those who *really* know me don't respect me, it means I'm not living right and doing what I should. Respect has to be earned. Keeping this in mind is a gut check for me and helps me remember to always do right by my family.

As parents, Margaret and I tried to give our children roots and wings. We gave them roots by instilling values that would keep them grounded. Today they have beautiful families and are giving their children those same roots. We also tried to give them a good self-image and believed in them so they could fly. Today we are also trying to do that for our grandchildren.

Here's what I know. You can't do much about your ancestors, but you can influence your descendants in a wonderful way.

Relationships

One of my strong beliefs, which I shared in my book *Winning with People*, is "All things being equal, people will do business with people they like. All things not being equal, they still will."

Success is a relationship game. Dr. Thomas W. Harrell, former professor emeritus of applied psychology at Stanford University, spent much of his career tracking a group of MBAs after graduation. He discovered that their grade point averages had little connection to their ultimate success in the business world. What really mattered was their social skills. The graduates who ended up with the most prestigious jobs and the highest salaries were communicative, outgoing, and energetic.[12] As New York–based executive recruiter John Callen says, "The most sought-after skill from CEO on down is the ability to communicate with people. The person who can do that in business will always be in demand."

> "The most sought-after skill from CEO on down is the ability to communicate with people."
> —John Callen

Relationships are important to every area of life. They help define who we are and what we can become. Most of us can trace our success to pivotal relationships.

Few things will pay you bigger dividends in life than the time and trouble you take to understand people and build relationships. As I have said for years, "People don't care how much you know until they know how much you care." Take care of relationships today, and you do much to take care of success tomorrow.

Mission

My mission, like yours, is personal. I am responsible for fulfilling mine. You are responsible for fulfilling yours. My personal mission is to add value to leaders who multiply value in others. Every day I have to ask myself whether I am actually doing that. I have never made it my goal to try to build companies or organizations. My passion has been for my mission and I have led organizations to try to fulfill it.

If I give personal attention to my mission every day, that will help to keep me from straying away from it someday in the future. That will also be true for you.

Health

The discipline of taking care of my health has been a daily battle for me. Eating right and exercising daily are things I find it very easy to neglect. And for many years I did. To me it looked like the only way to get healthy was to follow the advice of Mark Twain: "Eat what you don't want, drink what you don't like, and do what you'd druther not."

Though I don't have much natural desire in this area, I do possess a great desire to finish my life well—but not too soon. My cardiologist often says to me, "You help a lot of people and you are responsible for staying around as long as you can." So I work on my health daily. I may not do it perfectly, but I do it.

Each day is an unrepeatable miracle. Today will never happen again, so we must make it count. Do that with every today, and tomorrow will take care of itself.

> Each day is an unrepeatable miracle. Today will never happen again, so we must make it count.

7. Am I Investing My Time with the Right People?
A Question of ROI

The greatest legacy any leader can leave is the other leaders he raises up before he's finished. That means finding the right people and investing in them continually.

People often ask me how to find great leaders. The answer is simple: know what a great leader looks like. If you have a clear picture of a good leader and you can describe it in words, you know what you're looking for.

If you don't already have a list of your own, take a look at mine and see which factors you also desire in the leaders you work with:

1. **The Influence Factor**—Do they influence others?
2. **The Capacity Factor**—Do they have the potential to grow and develop?
3. **The Attitude Factor**—Do they desire to grow and develop themselves?
4. **The Chemistry Factor**—Do we like each other?

5. **The Passion Factor**—Are they self-motivated?
6. **The Character Factor**—Are they grounded?
7. **The Values Factor**—Are our values compatible?
8. **The Teamwork Factor**—Do they work well with others?
9. **The Support Factor**—Do they add value to me?
10. **The Creative Factor**—Can they find possibilities in impossibilities?
11. **The Option Factor**—Can their contribution give me options?
12. **The 10 Percent Factor**—Are they in the top 10 percent of those on our team?

When I first began developing leaders, I was so excited about making a difference with people that I was not very discriminating about whom I invested my time in. To put it bluntly, I recruited everybody. But then I discovered that not everyone desires to grow, and relatively few people truly want to make a difference. That's a problem, because you can't make a difference with people who don't want to make a difference.

You can make an equal investment of time, effort, and resources in two different people and you will get a completely different return on each. When I realized that different people gave different ROIs—returns on investment—I began to change the way I approached leadership development. I started to think about who had given a good return for my time and who hadn't. And that's when I began to define what a good leader looks like. When the picture became clear to me, my investments became strategic—and my results improved greatly.

What's on Your List?

Take some time to review my list and come up with your own. What factors are most important to you for selecting and investing in leaders? Remember, your leadership capacity and your legacy depend on the leaders you develop.

Author Noel M. Tichy says, "The ultimate test for a leader is not whether he or she makes smart decisions and takes decisive action, but whether he or she teaches others to be leaders and builds an organization that can sustain its success even when he or she is not around." That requires not only the intent to develop leaders, but also the right people who are willing and able to grow and develop.

These are the seven questions I ask myself as a leader every day—inspired by my conversation with Coach John Wooden. They help me to be successful by keeping myself growing, checking my motives, maintaining stability, promoting teamwork, leveraging my strengths, focusing on today, and investing in the right people. I hope my list inspires and encourages you to take some time and think about the questions you need to be asking yourself every day.

Socrates is quoted as saying, "The unexamined life is not worth leading." I would add that the unexamined leader is not worth following. Leaders who never take time to ask what they are doing and why they doing it are unlikely

> **The unexamined leader is not worth following.**

to stay on track, lead at their best, and reach their potential. That is why we need to keep asking ourselves tough questions.

3

What Questions Do I Ask My Team Members?

I f I were to ask you to picture great leadership moments, what kinds of things would come to mind? Do you envision leaders communicating inspirational messages to an audience, such as these?

"Never, never, never give up."—Winston Churchill

"Ask not what your country can do for you; ask what you can do for your country."—John F. Kennedy

"Mr. Gorbachev, tear down this wall."—Ronald Reagan

Or do you picture a leader on a battlefield, under fire and giving orders to his troops, maybe a general such as Robert E. Lee, George S. Patton, or Bernard Montgomery? Perhaps you think of an athlete taking control of a game and leading his team to victory, such as Michael Jordan, Joe Montana, or Lionel Messi.

All of those are valid leadership images. Leaders do often inspire others or take charge. But I want to give you another picture of leadership, one that's not as commonly envisioned. It's of a leader asking questions of team members and then really listening to what they have to say.

Unfortunately, many leaders don't automatically think of asking questions and listening as a leadership function. If they did, perhaps Coach John Wooden would not have asked, "Why is it so difficult to realize that others are more likely to listen to us if first we listen to them?" Those weren't mere words to Coach Wooden. They were backed up by his behavior. Whenever I spent time with him, I always felt that he wanted to listen to me more than he wanted to talk. He really wanted to know what I thought and how I felt. The man who was selected by *Sports Illustrated* as the greatest coach of the twentieth century led others by first listening to them.

Successful leaders don't only take action. Good leaders listen, learn, and then lead. Because I believe in that so strongly, I have worked to discipline myself to become a better listener. Though I often find it difficult, I try to follow the advice given by Robert Newton Peck: "Never miss a chance to keep your mouth shut."

> **"Never miss a chance to keep your mouth shut."**
> —*Robert Newton Peck*

How Good a Listener Are You?

If you want to become a better leader, you must become a better listener. And the way you listen matters. In their book *Co-Active Coaching*, authors Henry Kimsey-House, Karen Kimsey-House, Phillip Sandahl, and Laura Whitworth assert that there are three levels of listening.[13] Though their focus in the book is on listening for coaches, their observations are helpful for leaders. Here are the three levels of listening:

Level I: Internal Listening

The lowest level of listening is entirely focused on ourselves. We may be hearing information from others, but we pay attention only in terms of how we are affected by what the other person says. The authors write, "At Level I, the spotlight is on 'me': my thoughts, my judgments, my feelings, my conclusions about myself and others.... At Level I, there is only one question: *What does this mean to me?*"

This level of listening is obviously very limited. It can be appropriate while you're getting directions if you're lost, listening to a server recite the specials in a restaurant, or being given orders during an emergency. But it's not especially useful for leading others. For that, we cannot be focused only on ourselves and our own needs.

Level II: Focused Listening

If we engage with others at Level II, our focus changes from ourselves to the other people speaking. We tune in to not only their words, but also their emotions, inflection, facial expressions, posture, and so on. The authors call this the level of empathy, clarification, and collaboration. I might call it listening with emotional intelligence. In addition, the authors also point out that the listener is acutely aware of the impact that his or her response and interaction is having on the person speaking.

People capable of engaging at Level II are great conversationalists and good friends. People are attracted to them and respect them. This type of listening is a great skill to possess, yet there is another, higher level of listening.

Level III: Global Listening

This highest level of listening goes beyond just the speaker and listener. It takes into account the action, inaction, and interaction of the people involved, but it also takes in the environment and all that it entails. In addition, it relies heavily on the listener's intuition.

The authors point out, "Performers develop a strong sense of Level III listening. Stand-up comedians, musicians, actors, training presenters— all have the ability to instantly read a room and monitor how it changes in response to what they do. This is a great example of noticing one's impact. Anyone who is successful at influencing people is skilled at listening at Level III. These people have the ability to read their impact and adjust their behavior accordingly."

I would call Level III the listening level of effective leaders. They are able to read people, read the room, read the situation, and intuitively see what's coming. And if they're wise, they let all that information prompt them to ask increasingly penetrating questions.

Author and negotiation expert Herb Cohen explains, "Effective listening requires more than hearing the words transmitted. It demands that you find meaning and understanding in what is being said. After all, meanings are not in words but in people."

The Power of Listening

In the first chapter, I discussed the importance of questions. But what value is there to asking questions if you don't listen to the answers you receive? None. If you want to benefit from being a good questioner, you must become an even better listener. It has so many positive benefits, including these:

Listening Demonstrates That You Value Others

Author and professor David W. Augsburger says, "Being heard is so close to being loved, that for the average person, they are almost indistinguishable." Because that is true, when you listen to others you communicate that you care about them and value them.

> "Being heard is so close to being loved, that for the average person, they are almost indistinguishable."
> —David W. Augsburger

Audrey Moralez, one of the John Maxwell Team coaches I mentor, recently shared how being asked questions affects her. She wrote,

One of the things that strikes me most about John's questions is the fact that I have never felt so heard by a leader. Even though I am a newer member of the team, my thoughts matter and my opinions count. John's questions require me to think deeply about the ways that I can add value to the team, but what I value most is who I am becoming through the questions that are asked.

My mother unconditionally loved me like no other person in my life. As I reflect back on how she demonstrated that love to me, I can see that a constant that ran throughout my life was her desire to listen to me. Whether I was venting to her, crying about something that hurt me, sharing my dreams, or telling her a funny story, she always listened, and that translated into love for me.

Listening Has High Influence Value

One of the best ways to persuade others is with your ears. That may seem counterintuitive, because we expect persuasion to involve speaking. But when a leader listens to members of the team, that act gives the leader greater credibility and therefore influence. On the other hand, when team members no longer believe that their leader listens to them, they start looking around for someone who will.

Listening Leads to Learning

It's obvious that when you listen you can learn. But what's less obvious is that when you listen, you can help others learn. Mary Kay founder Mary Kay Ash asserted, "Listen long enough and the person will generally come up with an adequate solution." That's true because sometimes people need to talk something through to define the problem and find solutions.

Nothing is more satisfying to me as a leader than to watch my team find answers not through my words but through my ears. One of the greatest gifts I can give a person is the gift of attention.

> One of the best ways to persuade others is with your ears.

My Listening List

I have to confess that I have not always been a good listener. My wife Margaret would tell you that when we first got married, I talked too much and listened too little. I had a quick solution for every problem and was all too eager to share it. I took that same attitude into my professional life. But that attitude hurt me. I damaged some relationships because I didn't listen. And I often failed to benefit from the advice and ideas of those around me.

To combat this shortcoming, I had to take steps to become a better listener. I've improved in this area, but I still have to guard against talking too much and not listening enough. If you also need to do that, you may benefit from this list of questions that I developed to help myself to keep listening.

1. Do I Have an Open-Ear Policy?

High Point University president Nido Qubein believes, "Most of us tend to suffer from 'agenda anxiety,' the feeling that what we want to say to others is more important than what we think they might want to say to us." Do you find that to be true? I do. I must admit that I have acute "agenda anxiety." Members of my team can testify to the fact that I know where I'm going, I know how to get there, and I have a plan for how they can help me. It has taken me years to soften my natural inclination to direct others. How do I do that? As a leader I work to listen first, then lead.

2. Do I Interrupt?

Interrupting is impolite and is a symptom of an attitude problem. Have you ever gotten the feeling that the only reason another person is letting you talk is that they know they will get to speak next?

An engineering manager was asked his definition of teamwork. He said, "Teamwork is where everyone in the department is doing what I tell them without complaining." People with strong opinions or clear vision can have a tendency to cut to the chase, interrupt, and discount what others have to say. The problem is that interrupting translates to "What I want to say is more important than what you are saying."

> Interrupting translates to "What I want to say is more important than what you are saying."

3. Do I *Want* to Hear What I *Need* to Hear?

Hearing anything positive is easy. We all like good news. Everyone loves a compliment. But what about hearing something negative? How do you usually respond to bad news or criticism? Journalist Sydney J. Harris observed, "It is impossible to learn anything important about anyone until we get him or her to disagree with us; it is only in contradiction that character is disclosed. That is why autocratic employers usually remain so ignorant about the true nature of their subordinates."

Effective leaders encourage others to tell them what they need to hear, even when it's not what they want to hear. Max De Pree said, "The first responsibility of a leader is to define reality." That can happen only when the leader is willing to hear and face the truth.

Over the last thirty years I have been blessed to have two incredible assistants: Barbara Brumagin and Linda Eggers. I placed first Barbara and later Linda strategically at the center of communication in my organizations and empowered them to speak to me about anything they observed. They were often the people most aware of the total picture of the organizations I led. They knew what was important to me. Many times they've heard me say, "Tell me what I need to hear on the front end of a situation, not what you want to tell me or what you think I want to hear." It hasn't always been pleasant to receive negative news or feedback, but it has always helped me, the team, and the organizations.

My Questions for the Team

Listening is important for leaders, but if they don't ask the right questions, they're missing a lot. Good leaders ask great questions that inspire others to dream more, think more, learn more, do more, and become more.

> Good leaders ask great questions that inspire others to dream more, think more, learn more, do more, and become more.

I ask questions of my team continually. It has become a constant in my leadership that I do almost automatically both one-on-one and within groups. And my team has been shaped by those questions. Because I know they are so important to my personal leadership as well as the effectiveness of my organization, Margaret and I met with members of my team and inner circle one night recently to have dinner in a Buckhead (north Atlanta) restaurant. The goal was to talk about my process of asking questions and to identify the questions I ask my team all the time. At the table were Linda Eggers, my executive assistant; Charlie Wetzel, my writer; Stephanie Wetzel, my social media manager; Mark Cole, the CEO of my organizations; David Hoyt, my speaking agent and a company president; and Audrey Moralez, who does research and special projects for me.

We enjoyed a great dinner and had a fabulous discussion. Many of the questions we talked about carried special memories for us—times of laughter and tears, compromise and conviction, challenge and change. I've captured the highlights and will share them with you now. The questions are not listed in order of importance, but each question is important, because they have defined our team.

1. What Do You Think?

The question I ask most often has to be "What do you think?" These words come out of my mouth a dozen or more times every day. Mark Cole says that being asked this question does more for his leadership development than anything else we do. Mark explains, "When you ask for my skills, you get my strengths. When you ask for my passion, you get my heart. When you ask for my ideas, you get my mind. But when you ask me for answers, you get my strengths, heart, and mind."

"What do you think?" was the opening question I asked my team at the dinner we had together in Buckhead. I had requested that everyone come to the dinner with a list of questions I tend to ask. I also came with my own list. The first thing we did was look at my list so they could tell me what they thought. They immediately pointed out that one or two questions on my list were things none of them had ever heard me ask. I chuckled and crossed them off. Sometimes you don't actually do what you think you do. Instead we focused on the questions I actually do ask.

When I ask people what they think, at different times I do it for different reasons. I ask it for . . .

Gathering Information

Sometimes the question is as straightforward as it sounds. I simply want good information. Often I receive that from my inner circle, whom I value very highly. Every person is not only talented and capable, but also a good thinker. Often I ask what they think because I can learn from them. They are like an extension of me.

I believe that leaders see more than others see and see things before others do. Having leadership gifting is often like having a head start in a race. But obviously leaders don't see *everything*. By asking people on my team to tell me what they think, I can often gather additional information that gives me a better idea of what's going on. One of my jobs as a leader is to piece these bits of information together into a complete picture so I can make good decisions.

Confirming My Intuition

Often I have a strong sense that something is true, but cannot explain why. It comes out of a strong sense of intuition. We are all intuitive in our areas of strength; mine is most acute in leadership situations. If you think you know something, but you're not sure why, what can you do to validate your belief? Ask someone you trust. To verify that what I'm sensing is correct, I'll ask leaders I respect what they think. Their answers often put words to my feelings and confirm my intuition, giving me greater certainty as I plan or make decisions.

Assessing Someone's Judgment or Leadership

When new people join my team, I often ask what they think. For example, if we're in a meeting, I'll ask what they observed and get their opinion on what happened. It helps me learn if they read the room right. Or if we're strategizing, I'll ask how they think we should proceed. This is the fastest way to assess people's thinking and observation abilities.

Teaching People How I Think

Let me say one more thing about asking people what they think about an idea or subject. When I ask the question, I always tell people *why* I've asked it, because that is one of the best ways to teach people. *Why* is a great tool for connecting and equipping.

One of the best staff members I ever had was Dan Reiland. When I first met him, he was an intern at the church I led. He was so good that I hired him. Dan is not only a good leader, but also an exceptional developer of leaders. Every job I gave him, he did with excellence. He was so good, in fact, that I made him my executive pastor—roughly equivalent to the president of a company, if I had been the CEO and chairman.

When I asked Dan to serve in that capacity, I brought him in on a lot of my decisions, and I often asked him what he thought. Then I would tell him why I had asked and what I was thinking. Many times he understood the issues and the decision-making process. But other times he didn't. When that happened, he would come back and ask questions, and we would process the decision again until he understood it and would be able to make similar decisions for the organization himself in the future.

Processing a Decision

Sometimes people need a number of different perspectives in order to discover the best one. And sometimes they need time and reflection to process a decision. That has been true for me and for members of my team. Sometimes they have needed to move me along and convince me of a decision they believe in. Sometimes it's the other way around, and I need to give them time to come around. The give and take is very healthy.

While we talked about the "What do you think?" question over dinner, Charlie Wetzel, who's worked on my books with me for twenty years, asked how I know when to push for what I believe to be right and when to defer to members of the team. I explained that if I push for something my team doesn't agree with, I do so because I'm sensing an opportunity or because my leadership intuition about it is strong. That doesn't mean I run over my team or force the issue. It usually means that I give them time to process and that I revisit the issue multiple times so they can continue to receive additional information.

That's what happened in 2010 when Scott M. Fay and Paul Martinelli approached me about starting a coaching organization. When they first pitched the idea, I wasn't certain, but it didn't take me long to see the opportunities it presented for helping more people and creating a legacy. It took my inner circle longer to see those things. After the first time they met with Paul and me, I asked them, "What do you think?" They gave their feedback, but I could sense that they didn't yet see what I was seeing. That was OK. I gave them some time and then brought them back around to meet with Paul and me again. We did this three or four times before we got on the same page. And the results have validated my instincts. Today the John Maxwell Team has more than four thousand coaches and they are helping many people.

In contrast, there are times when I step back and defer to members of my inner circle. If a person is closer to the issue than I am, and he or she has a track record of success, I defer. Decisions should always be made as close to the problem as possible. If the team member is going to be responsible for carrying the endeavor

> **Decisions should always be made as close to the problem as possible.**

forward, I am more likely to defer. And if team members keep coming back with an idea or decision and do so with great passion, I am likely to reconsider my stance or decision and defer to them.

That was the case with the naming of The John Maxwell Company. When I decided to start a training, resourcing, and development company, I knew the direction I wanted the organization to go. But I wasn't sure what we should name it. The only thing I was certain of was that I did not want my name to be on it. But Mark Cole, who is now the CEO of the company, pushed back against that, citing the names of past organizations and initiatives I had led or founded: INJOY, ISS, Maximum Impact. "People saw those names and had no idea what those organizations did or that you were involved with them," Mark asserted. "If you want people to know what the new company will stand for, it has to have your name on it." Finally I relented. But I did insist on one thing: the word *company* needed to be much more prominent in the logo than my name.

I felt similarly about the John C. Maxwell Leadership Center. When Kevin Myers, the leader of 12Stone Church, approached me about naming the leadership center after me, I was reluctant to give my approval. I love Kevin and have mentored him for fifteen years. And I loved the idea of the leadership center and was thrilled to give it my endorsement. But I was uneasy about putting my name on it. I know how fallible I am. Kevin was persistent, and he eventually persuaded me that the profile and promotion this would bring to the organization should outweigh my reluctance.

Asking the question "What do you think?" has often allowed me to lead my organization better than I would have if I had relied only on myself. More than once, members of my team have saved me from making a bad or stupid decision because they saw things I didn't see, relied on experience I didn't have, or shared wisdom they possessed that I lacked. Their thinking has elevated my ability, and for that I am very grateful.

2. How Can I Serve You?

Years ago, when I frequently invited people to come and speak to members of my organization, I found there were two types of speakers. The first was those who were excited to be there and to get a chance to speak on a larger platform than they were accustomed to. They saw it as an opportunity to be on stage, to shine, and to receive recognition. The other type of person arrived with a mind-set to serve me and the organization. Before stepping out onto the platform, they wanted to know how they could help me and often asked, "Is there something I can say for you?" I was always glad to invite the second kind of speaker back.

Having speakers ask how they could help left a strong impression on me. I was already doing some speaking at that time, and I immediately began expressing my desire to help the people for whom I went to speak. Today I've taken that a step further. Before I speak for a client, I get on a conference call to ask questions. Often they defer to me, but I remind them, "I'm coming to serve you." And when we're in the greenroom prior to my going out onstage, I ask them the same question other speakers asked me: "Is there something I can say for you?"

As my team and I ate dinner and talked about the questions I ask them, they let me know how often I ask how I can serve them. My assistant Linda Eggers, who has worked with me for more than twenty-five years, said, "I can't remember a day that you didn't ask me if there was anything I needed to help me move forward." That's true. I never want to be the bottleneck for my team.

Charlie Wetzel commented, "When John and I talk or meet, one of the last things he asks me is whether there's anything he can do for me. That's not just a throwaway line. He genuinely wants to do whatever he can to help me get my work done quickly and easily. And he would do anything to help me personally too if I needed it."

I believe leadership is servanthood. It's my responsibility to make sure my people have what they need to succeed and get their work done. If you are a leader, that is your responsibility too. Asking, "How can serve you?" not only helps others, it also helps prevent me from developing a positional mind-set whereby I start thinking I'm somehow "over" or better than everyone else on the team.

There's another great benefit to asking your team this question: they ask it of the clients they serve. Recently David Hoyt told me that he asked this question of a client named Dianna. She responded by asking if there was any way David could introduce her to one of her heroes, Joel Osteen. David made it happen, and Dianna sent him a note that said, "Once again I am in awe. You just keep getting better. You inspire me. Love you."

Where Are You Holding Up Your Team?

If you are not asking the members of your team how you can serve them, you may be holding them up. To find out, go to each team member individually and ask, "What could I do for you that would make your job easier, make you more successful, and make the team better?" Listen without interrupting to what people have to say, and then try to figure out ways to do what you can to serve them.

---

3. What Do I Need to Communicate?

As a leader and speaker, I am often engaged in advance to communicate to an audience. As I've already explained, I find out as much as I can on a conference call before the event, and I ask my host if there's anything I can say to his or her people to help them. But sometimes I come in cold to a situation in which I am asked to speak. On such occasions I'll ask one of my inner circle, "What do I need to communicate?" Why? Because success in communication comes from knowing the context more than the content. When I ask this question, I'm not trying to find out what content to deliver. I'm trying to find out who the people are, what the situation is, what happened before I arrived to speak, and how I can connect and help them.

That was the case in January of 2013 as EQUIP launched its initiative to bring transformation to the country of Guatemala. My team and I traveled there so that I could speak to members of the seven streams of influence: business, government, education, family, media, the arts, and the church. In the course of a week, I communicated to more than twenty different groups: social activists; reporters and television hosts; teachers, professors, school administrators, and the secretary of education; priests, nuns, and pastors; leaders of the Mayan nation; entrepreneurs, businesspeople, and millionaires; and government employees, elected officials, and even the president of Guatemala. Some groups numbered in the thousands. Some meetings were with just a few people. It was the most exhausting and intensive week of my life.

My goal with every group or individual was the same: to connect. So as I left one meeting or event and traveled to the next, I got with Mark Cole and asked him, "What do I need to communicate?" I needed to know the context before I stepped into the room. Mark would tell me three things:

- Whom I would be talking to.
- What the most important thing was.
- What the call to action was.

Without Mark's help, I would have been in trouble. Knowing those three things made it possible for me to be successful. As a leader, you should not be trying to carry everything yourself. To be successful, you must share the load. But you must have highly capable people to hand things off to.

4. Did We Exceed Expectations?

One of the most important things you can do as a leader is make sure you and your organization are delivering what you promised. The question I ask to make an assessment of this is "Did we exceed expectations?" This ensures my future success and that of my organization. The future is dim professionally for anyone who doesn't exceed the expectations of customers or clients.

For me and my teams, meeting expectations is not enough. In everything we do, I want us to exceed what is expected. I insist on this for two reasons. First, I always want people to feel that they got *more* than their money's worth from me or the organizations I lead. Second, if we press to exceed expectations, it helps us to keep growing and improving. That's how we get to the next level.

One of the teachings I'm known for is the rule of five. Every day I read, write, think, ask questions, and file what I learn. These are the five disciplines I practice to keep improving. Recently the leaders of The John Maxwell Company decided that they wanted to develop a rule of five for the organization. They took some time to create their list of five disciplines and then showed it to me to get my feedback. Unfortunately, what they had produced was just average. That wasn't good enough. I asked them to keep working on it until they had something all of us could be proud of. I wanted them to exceed expectations.

If you want to be successful, you need to set the bar high for yourself and your team. It's not enough to simply finish a job. You need to perform it with excellence, without cutting any corners. Every time you bring something to completion, try to find out not only whether you were able to help, but *how much* you were able to help. If you make it your goal to exceed expectations, you can continue to learn, grow, and improve.

5. What Did You Learn?

When our children Elizabeth and Joel were growing up, whenever Margaret and I treated them to an experience or traveled with them, they knew I was going to ask them two questions: "What did you love?" and "What did you learn?" Sometimes when I'd ask them, they'd groan. But finding out what they loved helped us to connect with them and get to know them better, even when they were teenagers. And asking what they learned helped them to grow.

Elizabeth and Joel are now adults. They have gotten married to wonderful spouses and have children of their own. Elizabeth got her degree in education and trained to be an elementary school teacher.

Joel does sophisticated high-end technical installations of media and security systems for homes and businesses. His work requires him to travel quite a bit, which used to take him away from his wife Lis and their children. Joel's solution was to buy an RV and have the whole family travel together while he and Lis homeschool the children. To my great joy, Lis recently told me that as they travel and see the country, Joel keeps asking the children, "What did you love? What did you learn?"

The question "What did you learn?" is not just for parents with impressionable children. It's equally valuable in a work setting. I ask it all the time because it keeps my staff sharp and growing. It prompts people to evaluate their experience and make an assessment. And as I've often said, experience isn't the best teacher—*evaluated* experience is. Besides, I often also learn something when I hear people's answers; this question keeps me growing too!

> Experience isn't the best teacher—*evaluated* experience is.

David Hoyt has been part of my team for more than fifteen years. As I already mentioned, he is my speaking agent. Over dinner in Buckhead, as we talked about the questions I ask my team, David recounted the story of the first time he booked an international speaking engagement for me, many years ago. He handled all the details and worked with my host in Malaysia.

I arrived on-site and everything seemed great. However, when I got up in front of the audience and started to speak, I could tell that something wasn't right. The audience seemed detached and unresponsive. It was quite a struggle. It wasn't until after I was done that I found out why.

Weeks before, the host had asked David for my notes. Being helpful, he had sent a copy. David had assumed that the host would use them to promote the event. But what the host had done was print my notes—every word I planned to speak—and distribute them to everyone in attendance. Needless to say, the audience didn't respond the way I'd expected, because it knew what I was going to say before I said it!

Afterward David and I talked. And one of the questions I asked him was what he'd learned. "I learned never to do that again!" David joked as he told the story over dinner. "I also learned not to assume anything and to ask more questions."

A newer member of my team, Audrey Moralez, talked over dinner about how much she has learned by being invited to business meetings and conferences and then being asked, "What did you learn?"

"The first time John asked me this, I felt valued and included," said Audrey. "But it also made me accountable. The next time John invited me to something, I started to pre-think about what I would learn before the meeting. And I started evaluating and rethinking what I learned afterward. It's a great way to develop people."

Any time you ask an open-ended question like this one, you don't know what you will hear. The people who aren't inclined to learn and grow may not have much to say, but the sharp people shine. And they teach you something.

6. Did We Add Value?

My daily goal is to add value to other people. I want not only to make life better for my family, but also to encourage and reward the server at the restaurant where I eat lunch. I want members of my team to feel that the company and I do everything we can to help them succeed and improve every day. And I also want our clients and customers to feel we improved their situation and helped them to succeed, every time we come in contact with them. My desire in life is to add value to leaders who multiply value to others. That's why I ask this question.

That doesn't mean I always achieve this desire. Not long ago, at an event, I was signing books after speaking. I do this all the time, and my goal is to sign every book for every person who waits in line to see me. I shake hands, smile for pictures with people, and sign hundreds—sometimes thousands—of books.

This particular event didn't stand out to me as unusual. However, a few days after it, Linda made me aware of an e-mail she had received. It was from a man who had waited in the long line at the event and been frustrated with how I had treated him. He said I had been abrupt and rude. Wow! Not only had I not added value, I had actually devalued him. I felt terrible. So I asked Linda to get his phone number for me, and I called him to apologize.

I learned from that experience. It has helped me to do a better job when meeting people and signing books at speaking events. And any time I'm rushing too much and giving people too little, Linda gives me a gentle reminder to slow down and connect with people, for which I'm grateful.

7. How Do We Maximize This Experience?

One of my goals in life is to maximize every experience I have. In fact, "maximizing" is one of my top five strengths, according to StrengthsFinder. When I prepare for a learning lunch, I spend weeks doing research and formulating my questions. When I go to another country on vacation, I want to stay in the best location, eat at the best restaurants, find the best guide, visit the best sights, and learn as much as I can. When the company creates a product or service, I want to make it the best we possibly can and then help as many people as possible with it. When I see a business opportunity, I want to make the most of it in every way possible. And I want the members of my team to do the same.

At our dinner in Buckhead, Margaret told the story of how I made the most of my experiences when I turned sixty several years ago. Several months before my birthday, Margaret told me that it was going to be difficult for her to give me the party she knew I wanted. It would be nearly impossible to get all the people I wanted to invite together in the same place at the same time. "Besides," she insisted, "it's hard to surprise you." Just when I was about to give her five compelling reasons she should do it anyway, she said, "But I do have a solution. Have parties all year."

What a great idea! So that's what I did. I made the most of my experience of turning sixty. I took a group of people hunting. I took another group sailing. I took another group to see the Kentucky Derby. Every month I had a mini-party to celebrate with the people I love.

As we talked about my sixty celebrations, Mark and David recalled the trip we'd taken together to Ireland to play golf at Old Head Golf Links. We did lots of incredible things on that trip besides golfing, including taking a helicopter ride. But my favorite was eating dinner at the K Club, where the American Ryder Cup team had dined the year before. At that dinner I told each member of our group what he meant to me and how he had added value to my life. By the end we were all weeping. Mark said that dinner had been one of the top three experiences of his life. He explained,

> While at the table with an incredible and accomplished group of leaders, I was struck by what a privilege and honor that it was to be sitting there. We had just finished playing golf at one of top courses of the world and there was much to be grateful for. Then John did something that I had never experienced. We sat for three hours while John asked thoughtful and deep questions. As the night continued to unfold, the depth of relationship only grew between us. Time just stood still as John exposed a different and authentic way to influence high-level leaders by asking them to slow down and reflect. John's deep questions helped us drop the typical male barriers and leader posturing. He then went around the table and explained to each of us why he had invited us on that trip. He described the

influence and impact each person at the table had on him and explained what each meant to him personally, professionally, and relationally. That took the depth and authenticity to a whole new level. I had not seen John that vulnerable and appreciative before, and I linked that back to the questions that allowed each person to speak about themselves when answering.

I think we too often take opportunities and experiences for granted and don't make the most of them. That's a shame, because everything we do for others and every experience we have has so much potential. By asking how we can maximize our experiences, we make the most of them. Anything less and we're actually wasting parts of our lives.

> By asking how we can maximize our experiences, we make the most of them.

8. What Do I Need to Know?

For much of my life as a leader, I've maintained a very fast pace. Now that I'm approaching seventy years of age, when others expect me to slow down, I'm pressing on to make the most of my life while my mind is still sharp and I still have lots of energy. I want to finish well.

One of the ways I make the most of my time is to ask key people, "What do I need to know?" I've done that for years with Linda Eggers. I travel a lot and want to find out from perceptive people what's going on back in the office. Linda always has her finger on the pulse of everything happening in the company. She's aware of problems, knows how people are feeling, and can tell me what the atmosphere is in the office.

I often ask, "What do I need to know?" when I'm about to enter a meeting or engage in a phone call. It invites the team member to give me an overview of the situation, provide vital information, and prioritize what he or she believes will be most important. I will sometimes ask this question of several different people before an important meeting. For example, before a meeting with my publisher, I might ask it of Mark Cole to hear the priorities of the company, of my agents Sealy and Matt Yates to learn what's going on in the industry, of Charlie Wetzel to get his ideas on book content, and of Linda Eggers to be up to date on communication and other information. Each person's expertise, years of experience, and hours of work in his or her area help me to be at my best for the sake of the entire team. I always assume that others know something important I don't that will help me to lead and make decisions more effectively.

By far the person I ask this question of most at this season of life is Mark Cole. In fact, after our meeting at dinner, Mark felt so strongly about this question that he wrote an e-mail about it to us. He wrote,

> John asks me this question often when we have not talked for a few days. He also asks it after a significant business deal or decision has been made. He wants me to give him a 30,000 foot view of all of his companies, and he digs in only where he wants more information. This request for a briefing allows John to keep his focus on doing things that only he can do and yet get an overview or recap of what is happening in all of his companies and organizations in a quick synthesized form. It also lets him know that I'm keeping my eye on what really matters.
>
> When John asks this question and I answer, it helps him, but it also does a lot for me:
>
> ➤ It causes me to always be prepared by thinking through the big things that John wants and needs to know.
> ➤ It causes me to be succinct and specific about what matter[s] to me.
> ➤ It gives me a perspective over time on what matters most to John. When he asks about something I didn't give in an update, I learn more about what matters to him.

> ➤ It gives me a chance to express my challenges and get his input and viewpoint on it, often enabling me to see the bigger picture.
> ➤ It reassures me that I have access to my leader and he is backing me up.

Recently, John called me and asked, "What do I need to know?" He was traveling and out of the loop, so I hit the high points but also told him of some operational challenges one of his companies was having. I didn't want to tell him, but I did. He was frustrated by it, told me so, and communicated that I needed to get it resolved. But he also thanked me for telling him and assured me that he would rather hear about it from me first, so that he would be prepared when others told him about it.

The bottom line is that this question empowers me more than anything else John does for me or with me. It gets my head up out of the weeds, gives me perspective, and makes me a better leader!

The right questions asked of the right people help not only you but also them. Mark is a very secure leader, and for that reason he always tells me the truth. He's not afraid to give me bad news or to tell me that he doesn't understand something. And for those reasons, he keeps growing, and I love working with him.

9. How Do We Make the Most of This Opportunity?

I am entrepreneurial by nature. I like options. I seek out opportunities. And when I find them, I always want to make the most of them. Why? As I've already said, I'm a maximizer. But there is something more. The door to one opportunity often comes from another. If you pursue an opportunity, it almost always leads to other opportunities. People who wait for the *one* great opportunity often keep waiting. The way to find the best opportunities is to pursue the one at hand.

I've already mentioned how the John Maxwell Team came about and how we created The John Maxwell Company. I could see that starting both of these organizations would create many opportunities, but it has led to more than I had imagined. Paul Martinelli, president of the John Maxwell Team, is one of the best people I've ever known at making the most of opportunities. He is continually looking for ways to find and train more coaches, and he continually discovers ways to enhance their preparation process. For example, I recently mentioned to an audience how many leadership lessons I'd seen in Steven Spielberg's movie *Lincoln*, and how much I would love to teach those lessons to others using the movie. As I came off the platform, Paul already had a plan for me to teach it to the coaches who chose to attend the training event again. And when I did, it was a fabulous experience for those coaches.

My experience training the coaches prompted me to find other ways to maximize opportunities. Recently I picked three coaches to invest in so they could partner with The John Maxwell Company to pursue other opportunities. And I believe other coaches may do the same in the future. And my experience on coaching calls with the four thousand John Maxwell Team coaches caused me to want to do elite coaching with two other small groups of leaders, which we call the Circle and the Table.

If you are a leader, you cannot afford *not* to ask the question, "How do we make the most of this opportunity?" It may lead you to your best paths toward greater influence, innovation, and profitability for your team and organization.

10. How Are the Numbers?

Most people don't know this about me, but I love numbers and stats. I like to review them and analyze them. I'm naturally competitive and stats are like a scoreboard for me. So I'm constantly asking members of my inner circle, "How are the numbers?"

I want to know how many people are signed up to attend an event our company will put on. I want to know how many people will be attending an event I'm asked to speak at. I want to know the sales for the company every month. I want to know how many leaders EQUIP is training and what countries they're in. I want to know how many of each of my books has sold every month and what each one's lifetime sales are. Even if I won't like the numbers, I want to know them. It helps me to judge how I'm doing and to strategize for the future.

I've always been this way. When I started my career I used to pore over the annual reports put out by my organization. But I have to admit I haven't always enjoyed looking at financial figures. My brother Larry once took me to task for that, because a leader who has vision and a team but no way to pay for them won't be successful. I'm a better leader because of it.

Mark Cole is the person I ask most often for numbers. He can tell me what's going on at The John Maxwell Company and EQUIP. He knows what new deals we're working on. Whenever I ask for numbers, he knows them. And Mark says it actually helps him too. Here's what he has to say about it:

> When John asks me for numbers, it actually does a lot for me. First, it keeps my head in the game and keeps me accountable. I am constantly on top of the details so that I'm prepared to talk about the numbers with him.
>
> His asking about the numbers also demonstrates to me that no matter our role in the company—from CEO to front-line worker—everyone needs to keep an eye on performance indicators.
>
> Finally, it drives me every day to perform better and to empower the team to perform better so that everyone is successful and we can give a good report to our boss.

Numbers count. They tell a story. They let you know what the score is. They show you where you're winning and where you're failing so you can make adjustments. They show trends. They reveal weaknesses. They are tangible evidence of how well you're doing.

What Numbers Do You Need to Know?

If you're a leader, there are numbers that are important for the success of your team and organization. Have you identified them? Talk to team members. If you work for others, ask them. Figure out which numbers matter and how often you need to be updated on them. Then make it a part of your regular discipline to . . .

Review the numbers.
Assess where you are succeeding and falling short.
Make changes to improve yourself, your team, and your organization.

If you don't already do this, it will improve your leadership dramatically.

---

11. What Am I Missing?

There's one last question I often ask: "What am I missing?" In fact, it is the question I ask most frequently, after "What do you think?" Why? I'm very aware that I don't always catch everything that's being explained to me or going on around me. Sometimes I can sense that everyone in a conversation seems to get something that's being said, but I still don't. Others are willing to help me get on the same page if I'm willing to ask.

Two of the fastest ways to connect with another person are to ask questions and to ask for help. Most people genuinely want to help others. And most people enjoy being an expert in their field and sharing their wisdom and experience. The only time these things don't seem to be true is in an environment that discourages asking genuine questions and listening to honest answers.

> **Two of the fastest ways to connect with another person are to ask questions and to ask for help.**

How to Create an Environment That Values Questions

Creating an environment where people are willing to ask and answer questions leads to high morale and positive results. Here's how you can do that:

- **Value each team member:** When leaders ask questions and really listen, they show that they value others. Sam Walton said, "Asking and hearing people's opinions has a greater effect on them than telling them, 'Good job.'"
- **Value questions more than answers:** Essayist Joseph Joubert asserted, "It's better to debate a question without settling it than to settle a question without debating it." Questions lead to thinking and discussion. The process is often more valuable than the answer.
- **Value the potential of your team:** When I sit with my team, the first thing I do is eliminate positional authority and divisions. I value contribution much more than title or tenure.
- **Value the improvement of a good idea:** Great ideas are a result of several good ones put together. Let everyone at the table know that the best idea will be the one we embrace.

Author C. S. Lewis said, "The next best thing to being wise oneself is to live in a circle of those who are." You can do that by creating a positive environment for questions.

One of my greatest joys is that members of my inner circle have taken this practice of asking questions and begun to use it with their families. David Hoyt told me that he recently took his daughter Gracie

> "Asking and hearing people's opinions has a greater effect on them than telling them, 'Good job.'"
> —Sam Walton

on a trip to Spain when he was speaking for EQUIP. Not only did David do everything he could to maximize the experience for her by taking her to cathedrals, visiting palaces, going to museums, taking her to a flamenco show, and wandering through the city with her, but he also asked her insightful questions as they ate dinner together.

And Mark Cole has told me that he uses the family dinner table as a place to regularly ask questions of his family. He says that sometimes the questions he and his wife ask are crazy and irrelevant, sometimes strategic and intentional. Mark says, "The questions allow our daughters to discover life truths and personal values. We ask questions that cause us to dream and questions that cause us to reflect." When Mark recently asked, "What is the one thing you most enjoy that we do as a family?" his seven-year-old daughter Macy responded, "Asking questions at the dinner table!"

Give Birth to Great Questions

The evening at dinner I spent asking questions of my team wasn't unusual for me. There is nothing I enjoy more than wonderful food paired with conversation. Give me an evening with friends talking about interesting subjects and I'm in heaven. The key to those magical evenings is good questions. My friends know that when I ask them to dinner, there will be two menus: one for food and one for our conversation, in the form of questions. Often as we head to dinner my guests will ask me, "John, what are the questions for tonight?" I try never to disappoint them.

Recently Audrey Moralez sent me an e-mail in which she wrote,

It's said that Socrates was the midwife of man's thoughts. The assumption is, of course, that people are pregnant with ideas and that they simply can't deliver them on their own. They need a little help from the midwife. Interestingly, I think this is exactly what good thinkers should be able to do. Unfortunately, many people that are intelligent are more academic than practical and more concerned about internal value than external value. They seem to believe that if they hold on to valuable thoughts that it makes them more valuable. Their self-worth seems to be tied up in knowing more than everyone else.

What I appreciate about you and other members of the John Maxwell Company is the fact that it doesn't matter how good the idea is; if it doesn't get born and start running around on its own two feet, then it wasn't a very good idea at all. Good ideas must be shared, improved upon with the help of other good thinkers, and then they must be implemented and acted upon. John, I think of you as a midwife.

What Audrey is describing is an environment where questions are valued and the answers of the team make a difference. I think that's what every good leader wants if he's willing to let go of his ego, get over his insecurities, and realize that only a team working together wins anything of value.

If you lead a team, start asking questions and *really* listening. Start valuing the contributions of your teammates ahead of your own. And remember that when the best idea wins, so does the entire team.

PART II

Questions Leaders Ask Me

Great Questions

I trust you are starting to get a feel for how important questions are to good leaders. I have yet to meet a great leader who didn't ask insightful and probing questions. The best leaders know that questions open doors for good leadership, promote great collaboration, and bring about solid teamwork.

If your goal is to be the best leader you can be, I hope you are already asking yourself the tough questions leaders must ask to be successful. And I hope you're asking every member of your team strategic questions continually. Remember, you get answers only to questions you ask.

When my team and I first started to discuss *Good Leaders Ask Great Questions*, I knew I wanted to help you become a better leader not only by teaching you how to ask better questions, but also by answering some of the most common and pressing leadership questions I frequently get asked.

As I mentioned in the opening of chapter one, people at conferences and events ask me questions all the time. But I wanted to open the door to questions even wider. So I asked Stephanie Wetzel, my social media manager, to solicit people's questions via Twitter, Facebook, and my blog. We also invited my four thousand John Maxwell Team–certified coaches to ask questions.

In only days we received hundreds upon hundreds of great questions, ranging from the basic to the sophisticated. The team and I spent weeks going through them, categorizing them, and selecting what would be the most helpful to leaders. I then set about writing the chapters by answering every question. You'll find that each of the following chapters begins with a list of the questions that were asked on the subject, in the order in which they are answered.

As you read, I believe you will find the most practical and useful leadership advice I've ever given. Some of the answers I give will affirm your leadership instincts. I hope many others will provide you with new insights and stir your thinking. Maybe they will prompt you to begin asking more leadership questions yourself and exploring new areas of growth. My goal is to jump-start your leadership skills and help you develop your leadership potential.

A Special Thank You

I would like to thank the hundreds of people who asked questions for this book and especially the following individuals whose great questions appear in the following chapters. The answers given are only as good as the questions asked. If this book serves people well, it is because of the quality of your questions.

Farshad Asl*

Andrew Axon

Rudolf Bakkara

John Barrett*

Art Barter

Betsi Bixby*

David Cipura

Beckie Cisler

Brandon Cockrell

Mark Cole

Jose Cordova

Anthony Coyoy

John DeWalle

David Emmanuel

Andre Finley

Aaron Frizzelle

Arnulfo Jose Suarez Gaeke

Brittany Gardner

Suvasish Ghosh

George Gomes

Ralph Govea

Deja Green

Virginia Gronley*

Charles Grubb

Penny Guinnette

Dean Haberlock

Peter Harding

Nathan Hellman

Eric Herrick

David Igbanoi

Loh Jen-Li Jenline

Osia Jerry

Laura Lambert

Rick Lester*

Lynette Little

Trudy Menke*

Benedick Naceno

Lusanda Ncapayi

Cyril Okeke

Rick Olson

Jenny Pace

Marc Pope

Lister Rayner

Dan Reiland

D. Roberts

Lynsey Robinson

Monika Patricia Rohr

Diane Runge

Amine Sahel

Vanessa Sanchez*

Eileen Schwartz*

Israel Silva*

Barry Smith*

David Specht

Sarah Stanley

David Stone

Timothy Teasdale*

Elias Tona

Jason Viergutz

Mike Walt

Misty West

Jeff Williams

Dale Witherington

Fernando Zambrano*

---

* Denotes John Maxwell Team Coach

Questions Related to How People Can Lead Themselves Successfully

1. Why does leading myself seem more difficult than leading others?
2. What gives a leader sustainability?
3. What are the most important values for a leader?
4. What is the most effective daily habit for any leader to develop?
5. How does one change one's heart to increase the desire to add value to and serve others?
6. If I am reaching goals and achieving success, why should I take care of developing myself as a leader?
7. How do you lead with humility when in the tough corporate world it's viewed as a weakness?
8. How transparent should a leader be? Is it OK for the team to know of personal challenges, such as cancer?
9. The leadership process is a long journey—lasting a lifetime. How can I overcome the loneliness I sometimes feel?
10. How can leaders develop the ability to "filter" their emotions to make good leadership decisions?

4

What Must I Do to Lead Myself Successfully?

When we began talking to my Twitter followers, Facebook fans, and John Maxwell Team coaches about the importance of questions, and we asked them to give me leadership questions that they wanted answered, we were flooded with questions related to self-leadership. We got more on this subject than any other. The next-largest category had less than half as many questions. Why so many? I think many people understand intuitively that if you can't lead yourself effectively, everything else in your life will be a struggle.

Self-leadership comes first. It makes every other kind of leadership possible. In *The 5 Levels of Leadership*, I explain that the Level 1 Position is the lowest level of leadership, the entry level. People on that level of leadership try to use their title and their rights to get others to follow them, rather than trying to develop genuine influence. But for even that lowest of leadership levels to remain valid, it must be built on a solid foundation of self-leadership. That's where personal credibility is established.

As you read through this chapter, I encourage you to think about how well you lead yourself—even if you are a seasoned high-level leader. Some of the challenges you face may come from the way you lead yourself. You may attribute them to someone or something else, when you actually need to look at yourself as the source. And as you'll see from the first question, no one is immune from this problem.

1. Why Does Leading Myself Seem More Difficult than Leading Others?

One of the reasons we have such difficulty leading ourselves is that we have blind spots preventing us from seeing where we have problems and fall short. My friend Larry Stephens recently sent me an e-mail on this subject. He wrote,

> It's my perception that almost everyone has a blind spot. Watching the news and reading the WSJ in particular [I've noticed] there have been so many leaders in recent years that have been cut down by what may have been their blind spot. They just somehow didn't see it coming.... It's my perception that TBS [the blind spot] defies a single definition or category. A character flaw might be a blind spot, but not necessarily so. It might be an addiction, a weakness, ego, innocence, failure to pay attention to details, but then it might not be any of them at all.

What are blind spots? They are areas in which people continually fail to see themselves or their situation realistically. Everybody has some; few people recognize their own. In fact, that was the first lesson they taught in a counseling course I took in college. We see others more clearly than we see ourselves. Why? Because we see ourselves by our intentions.

> **What are blind spots? They are areas in which people continually fail to see themselves or their situation realistically.**

That often gives us a false impression of who we are or what we do. We give ourselves the benefit of the doubt because we put things into context. On the other hand, we see others in light of their actions. For that reason we seem to be more objective when judging them.

While blind spots cause all people problems, they can be especially harmful in leaders. Because leaders influence others and their actions affect a team's, department's, or organization's outcomes, the problems that come from their blind spots are exaggerated. Their blind spots have a multiplying effect on the people in their sphere of influence.

To lead yourself successfully, you must identify your blind spots and deal with them effectively. To help you do that, I want to talk about the four most common and destructive blind spots among leaders:

1. A Singular Perspective

I must admit that this was one of my blind spots early in my career. My attitude could have been summed up by the motto "Save time— see it my way!" My opinions were strong and I always thought I was right. What I didn't realize was that I wasn't practicing good leadership when I tried to force people to see things my way, because I alienated people. Equally bad was that I was missing out on valuable input from others who had something to contribute. As Larry Stephens says, "If the only tool you have is a hammer, you tend to see every problem as a nail." I was the hammer and everyone else was a nail.

Having too singular a perspective might be a problem for you if...

• **No matter how a conversation begins, you end up talking about your favorite subject.** People with a singular focus tend to turn the conversation to their favorite subject and can be very creative about getting there—even when others see no logical connection.

- **You keep giving the same speech, lecture, or piece of advice over and over again.** If you're overly focused on a single concern, you may keep coming back to your favorite bit of advice and not even be aware of it.
- **You are always right.** Nobody is always right—on any subject. If you think you are, your focus is too narrow and you aren't even aware of it.

Instead of viewing everything from such a singular perspective, effective leaders make an effort to see things from different points of view. They are like Art Mortell, who noted, "I love playing chess. Whenever I'm losing at chess, I consistently get up and stand behind my opponent and see the board from his side. Then I start to discover the stupid moves I've made because I can see it from his viewpoint. The salesperson's challenge is to see the world from the prospect's viewpoint."[14] That's the leader's challenge too.

One of my favorite stories about perspective involves a general and a young lieutenant on a train in England after World War II. The only seats available to them were across from a beautiful young woman and her grandmother. After they had been riding awhile, the train went through a long tunnel where everyone was in total darkness for about ten seconds. In the silence the four passengers heard two things: a kiss and a slap.

Everyone had their own perceptions as to what had happened.

The young lady thought to herself, "I'm flattered that the lieutenant kissed me, but I'm terribly embarrassed that Grandmother hit him!"

The grandmother thought, "I'm aggravated that he kissed my granddaughter, but I'm proud she had the courage to defend her honor!"

The general thought, "My lieutenant showed a lot of guts in kissing that girl, but why did she slap me by mistake?"

The lieutenant was the only one on the train who really knew what had happened. In those moments of darkness he had the opportunity to both kiss a pretty girl and slap a general.

2. Insecurity

Insecure leaders continually think of themselves first. They worry about what others think of them. They fear that they may look weak or foolish or insignificant. Insecure leaders take more from people than they give. Because they feel they are less, they seek validation more. As a result, their teams and organizations suffer because others' best interests are overlooked in favor of the insecure leader's best interests.

Insecure leaders also limit their best people. They have a difficult time seeing others rise because it threatens them. And they cannot genuinely celebrate the victories won by others because they are often jealous. Giving others their due makes them feel like less.

Because insecurity is often hidden in a blind spot, leaders often don't recognize it in themselves. How do you know if insecurity is a problem for you? Answer the following questions:

• **Do you have a hard time giving credit to others?** Insecure people *need* credit, so it irks them to share it. Industrialist Andrew Carnegie noted, "No man will make a great leader who wants to do it all himself or get all the credit for doing it."

• **Do you keep information from your staff?** Withholding information is withholding trust. It's protecting your position. In contrast, when you give others information, you empower them. You communicate your trust and confidence in them.

• **Do you try to keep your staff away from good leaders?** If you worry that a good leader will "steal" your people, that is a sign of insecurity.

• **Are you threatened by the growth of others?** If it bothers you when others grow in knowledge and position, you may be an insecure leader.

• **Do you often micromanage others?** Insecure leaders want to have tight reins on everyone and everything. They may say they do it to ensure the outcome, but deep down they also desire to take credit for everything.

> "Nothing is a greater impediment to being on good terms with others than being ill at ease with yourself."
> —*Honoré de Balzac*

In the end, insecure leaders limit their people and their organization. As French novelist Honoré de Balzac observed, "Nothing is a greater impediment to being on good terms with others than being ill at ease with yourself."

3. An Out-of-Control Ego

Another major blind-spot area for leaders is ego. English artist and critic John Ruskin said, "Pride is at the bottom of all great mistakes."

> "Pride is at the bottom of all great mistakes."
> —*John Ruskin*

I don't know about *all*, but it sure creates many problems. Egotistical leaders believe they know it all. They believe others are inferior to them. And they often think the rules don't apply to them.

Egotistical leaders are usually rigid and closed-minded. They are out of touch with their clients and employees, they blame others when anything goes wrong, and they live in a state of denial. Their only positive quality is that they don't talk about others—because they never think about anyone but themselves.

Here are some warning signs that you might be an egotistical leader:

• **Do you think no one else can do a job as well as you can?** Egotistical leaders believe they are indispensible.

• **Are others always to blame when things go wrong?** Leaders with ego issues refuse to accept responsibility for wrongdoing, and place the blame on others.

• **Do you disregard the ideas of others?** Egotistical leaders dismiss others' ideas as inferior to their own.

• **Do other people often feel put down by you?** The superior attitude and insensitivity of egotistical leaders often makes other people feel insulted or dismissed.

Egotistical leaders don't look for input or answers from anyone other than themselves.

4. Weak Character

When you ask most people what it takes to be successful, they list talent, opportunity, and hard work as the primary ingredients. While those things are essential, so is character. Why? Character protects your talent. With character, all those other attributes help a leader to be successful. Lack of character is a deal-breaker when it comes to leading yourself or others. Character is the sum total of all our everyday choices. It is putting right values into action every day. It's consistency of values, ideals, thoughts, words, and actions.

If you suspect that character weaknesses may be holding you back, note your answers to these questions:

- **Do you often miss deadlines?**
- **Do you make vows, resolutions, or decisions to change and then go back to your old behavior?**
- **Do you place more importance on pleasing others than you do on maintaining the values you espouse?**

- **Are you willing to shave or shade the truth in order to get out of a tough spot?**
- **Do you do what's easiest, even when you know it's not what's best?**
- **Do others show reluctance to trust you?**

If you answer yes to any of these questions, there may be areas of your character that need some work.

How to Overcome Your Blind Spots

1. **Assume that you have blind spots.** If you don't believe that you have blind spots, that *is* your blind spot!

2. **Ask those who know you best to identify your blind spots.** If they are honest, they will tell you what you aren't seeing about yourself.

3. **Assume your blind spots cannot be removed by you alone.** Everyone needs help seeing and dealing with blind spots. Don't think you can deal with yours on your own.

4. **Openly discuss your blind spots with your inner circle.** Be open with the people who care about you and want to help you.

5. **Develop and empower a team to cover your blind spots.** You may eventually be able to overcome many of your blind spots. Until then, make sure your team prevents them from derailing you or the team.

In his book *American Scandal*, Pat Williams tells the story of Mahatma Gandhi's trip to England to speak for Indian independence before Parliament. Gandhi had often been threatened, arrested, and jailed because of his outspokenness, but that didn't silence him. Before Parliament, Gandhi spoke eloquently and passionately for nearly two hours, after which the packed hall gave him a standing ovation.

Afterward a reporter asked Gandhi's assistant, Mahadev Desai, how the Indian statesman had been able to deliver such a speech without any notes.

"You don't understand Gandhi," Desai responded. "You see, what he thinks is what he feels. What he feels is what he says. What he says is what he does. What Gandhi feels, what he thinks, what he says, and what he does are all the same. He does not need notes."

When values, thoughts, feelings, and actions are in alignment, a person becomes focused and his character is strengthened. That allows a leader to lead himself successfully.

2. What Gives a Leader Sustainability?

The question itself implies that leaders don't always last. They get tired. They get off track. They become discouraged. They lose momentum. All those things are true, because leadership isn't easy.

Every day, leaders must wake up and lead themselves before they lead anyone else. Because other people are depending on them, they must keep the fire burning within themselves. They must know where they're going, know why they're going, and help others get there. To stay energized and on course, leaders can sustain themselves by tapping into four areas:

1. Passion

Passion gives you two vital leadership characteristics: energy and credibility. Pioneering aviator Charles Lindbergh said, "It is the greatest shot of adrenaline to be doing what you have wanted to do so badly. You almost feel like you could fly without the plane." When you love what you do and do what you love, others find it inspiring. How many people do you know who became successful at something they hate?

Columnist Whit Hobbs wrote, "Success is waking up in the

morning, whoever you are, wherever you are, however old or young, and bounding out of bed because there's something out there that you love to do, that you believe in, that you're good at—something that's bigger than you are, and you can hardly wait to get at it again today." That's what passion does for a leader.

2. Principles

Successful leaders stay true to their principles—to their beliefs, gifts, and personality. They don't try to lead in a style that does not suit who they are. If they ask themselves, "Is my leadership style comfortable and does it reflect who I truly am?" they can answer with a resounding yes!

It takes time for leaders to know themselves. People often ask me about my communication style, and I let them know it took me eight years to find my way and become myself onstage. It's also taken me time to develop my leadership style. But I can only be at my best when I am being true to myself. The better you know yourself and the more true you are to yourself, the greater your potential for sustainable success.

3. Practices

Nearly anyone can achieve flash-in-the-pan success. We all get lucky from time to time. But if we want to sustain success—as an individual or a leader—we need to implement right and regular practices that help us to do the right thing day after day.

Successful people do daily what unsuccessful people do occasionally. They practice daily disciplines. They implement systems for their personal growth. They make it a habit to maintain a positive attitude. At the very least, these things keep their personal momentum going. At their very best, they make every day a masterpiece.

Identify and Implement Your Own Daily Practices

Leaders need to identify their own principles-based practices that will help them to remain passionate, true to themselves, and engaged with their team. Here is my list, which I call my daily dozen:

Just for today...
I will choose and display the right attitudes.
I will determine and act upon important priorities.
I will know and follow healthy guidelines.
I will communicate with and care for my family.
I will practice and develop good thinking.
I will make and keep proper commitments.
I will earn and properly manage finances.
I will deepen and live out my faith.
I will accept and show responsibility.
I will initiate and invest in solid relationships.
I will plan for and model generosity.
I will embrace and practice good values.
I will seek and experience improvements.

Taken from *Today Matters*.

4. People

The final factor in sustainability for leaders is the team. The people around you will either wind you up or wear you down. Ideally everyone would lead a great team, have fantastic friends, maintain a strong inner circle, and possess a loving family. Many leaders don't have all these. If

> The people around you will either wind you up or wear you down.

that's the case for you, don't be discouraged. Even if you have only one person in your corner cheering you on, you can still lead successfully.

Meanwhile, work to bring positive supportive people around you. Look for...

- **Believers:** People who believe in you and your vision.
- **Achievers:** People who contribute to the team with excellence.
- **Conceivers:** People who bring good ideas to the table.
- **Relievers:** People who complement your skills and abilities.

I believe that no leader ever needs to burn out. There have been many times in my life when I've gotten tired or frustrated or discouraged. But I'm sixty-six years old, I've been leading for more than forty years, and I'm still excited every day about life's endless possibilities. You can be too. Just remember to tap into your passion, stay true to your principles, implement the right practices, and surround yourself with the right people.

3. What Are the Most Important Values for a Leader?

All individuals have to decide what values they will embrace, what they will live for, what they would die for. Those values come from their core beliefs and their faith. I won't address those here, because I believe you must wrestle them down personally. Instead I'll talk about the *leadership* values that I believe are most important.

Servanthood: Leading Well Means Serving Others

People want to lead for many reasons. Some want power. Others seek riches. Many are driven by an ideology or a desire to change the world. I believe the only worthy motivation for leadership is a desire for servanthood. I love what Eugene B. Habecker writes in *The Other Side of Leadership*:

The true leader serves. Serves people. Serves their best interests, and in so doing will not always be popular, may not always impress. But because true leaders are motivated by loving concern, rather than a desire for personal glory, they are willing to pay the price.[15]

If you want to lead others but you are unwilling to serve people, I think you need to check your motives. If you are willing to embrace servanthood, not only will you become a better leader, you will help your team, help the people your team serves, and make the world a better place.

Purpose: Let Your *Why* Direct Your *What*

I believe that success comes from knowing your purpose in life, growing to your maximum potential, and sowing seeds to benefit others. If you miss any one of those three things, I don't think you can be genuinely successful. I also know that you cannot achieve the second and third parts fully without first discovering the first. You can't grow to your potential if you don't know your purpose. And if you don't know why you're on this earth and you are not able to improve in that purpose to the best of your ability, you'll be very limited in the ways you can help others.

I answer questions about discovering your purpose in chapter nine, so I won't go into that here. I'll just say that once you understand your purpose, you need to prioritize your life according to that purpose. If you don't, you'll continually get off track and you may never feel a real sense of fulfillment and completion.

Integrity: Live the Life Before You Lead Others

Too many leaders are like bad parents. They do whatever they want and tell the people they are supposed to be leading, "Do as I say, not as

I do." That doesn't work in parenting or in leadership. Why? Because people do what people see!

Great teams are made up of people with diverse skills. But when it comes to values, habits, disciplines, and attitudes, there needs to be unity. That starts with the example set by the leaders. If the leaders are undisciplined, the people will follow suit. If they come to work late, fail to hit their budgets, do sloppy work, waste time, and treat people poorly, guess what their people will do?

When you become a leader, you must focus more on your responsibilities than on your rights. You must raise your standards. You must do more than you expect of others. If you live the life first and lead well, others will respect you. And the chances are good that they will be willing to follow you.

> When you become a leader, you must focus more on your responsibilities than on your rights.

Relationships: Walk Slowly Through the Crowd

Leadership impact is drawn not from position or title but from authentic relationships. How do you develop authentic relationships? You live with authenticity. You treat people with kindness and respect. And you go to where they are to connect with them.

A lot of leaders wait for their people to come to them. They assume that people will come to them if they need or want something. But good leaders don't think that way. Effective leaders initiate. They communicate vision. They seek out opportunities. They start initiatives that will benefit the organization. And they initiate with people too. They know that they will never possess what they are unwilling to pursue. They want good relationships with the people who work with them, so they seek those people out. They ask them questions. They learn who they are. They offer assistance. They find ways for them to succeed. If you want to become a better leader, become highly relational.

Renewal: Replenish Yourself Daily

Life is demanding. People are demanding. The more you lead and the more you succeed, the more others will expect from you. If you don't make an effort to replenish your energy, feed your soul, and renew your mind, you will run out of gas. Replenishing yourself requires your attention. You have to be intentional about it.

Stephen Covey, author of *The 7 Habits of Highly Effective People*, called this "sharpening the saw" and described it as "preserving and enhancing the greatest asset you have—you. It means having a balanced program for self-renewal in the four areas of your life: physical, social/emotional, mental, and spiritual."[16]

What Renews You?

How do you go about renewing yourself daily, weekly, monthly, yearly? What renews your energy? What feeds your soul? What gives you emotional strength? What renews and improves your mind? Identify those things.

What rhythms of life have developed for you? How does your energy ebb and flow? When do you need renewal? Learn those rhythms and schedule activities to help you remain sharp. Fatigue can be costly.

Certainly there are other important values for leaders, but these are the ones I put at the top of my list. I encourage you to examine your own core beliefs and decide which values are most important to you.

4. What Is the Most Effective Daily Habit for Any Leader to Develop?

If you could cultivate only one habit to practice every day of your life, I believe it should be this: giving more than you receive. I say that because having a giving mind-set has so many benefits:

Giving Acknowledges That Others Have Helped Us

No one succeeds in life on his own. Every one of us has been helped along the way by other people. When we give to others, we acknowledge that by paying it forward.

Giving Requires Us to Get Beyond Ourselves

When your mind-set is to give more than you take, it forces you to think of others more than of yourself. You have to pay attention to others and what they want. You have to figure out how to give it to them. These things shift your focus from yourself to others. That very fact makes you less selfish.

> When your mind-set is to give more than you take, it forces you to think of others more than of yourself.

Giving Is by Nature Intentional

People rarely give by accident. They must make an effort to give. It is an act of will. That intentionality grows us and makes us more proactive—important qualities for leaders.

Giving Changes the World—One Person at a Time

What would the world be like if everyone tried to give more than he or she took? People would change. It's difficult for a healthy person to keep receiving from others without giving something back. Out of abundance comes generosity. Give generously to others without the hope of return, and the person receiving is changed and wants to pass it on. Once you have the mind-set of giving, the more you receive, the more you want to give. It becomes a positive cycle. As it spreads, not only do individuals change, but so do communities.

What does this have to do with leadership? How do you respond to people who give? How do you respond to generous leaders? Don't their actions make you want to give back, work harder, do your best? I know that's what they do for me. If you become a generous leader who always strives to give more than you receive, you will create a positive team and organization that others will always want to be a part of.

Three Questions to Ask Before You Can Effectively Give More

1. **What have you been given?** Look back on your life and think about what you've been given. Even people from the least advantaged backgrounds have positive experiences to draw upon.

2. **What do you have?** Look within to discover what talents, skills, and passions reside in you that you can pass along to others. You have worth. Others can benefit from your time and expertise.

3. **What can you do?** Chances are that there are things you can do for others right now. Look around you. What opportunities do you currently see to add value to others?

---

5. How Does One Change One's Heart to Increase the Desire to Add Value to and Serve Others?

I understand that not everyone is a people person. I'm an extrovert and I have always enjoyed being around people. So I went into leadership loving people, but I was pretty naïve. When I hired my first staff member, I loved him and mentored him and poured myself into him. Everything seemed great, and I figured we would ride into the sunset together like the Lone Ranger and Tonto. But then he violated some major leadership trust issues and I had to fire him.

That was really hard for me. And to be quite frank, it really hurt and I felt sorry for myself. I remember thinking, *How could this happen? How could he do this to me?*

That's when I made a decision: the next time I hire people, I will not let them get close to me. I'll give them jobs, let them know what I expect, and keep my distance. I'll tell them, "You do your job, and I'll do my job. See you in December at the Christmas party." And that's what I did. The next time I hired a staff member, I laid out my expectations in clear cold language and turned him loose. I left him alone for six months. And the good news was that he never hurt me. But the bad news was that he never really helped me either.

You can't be an effective leader by keeping people at arm's length. You can't mentor them if you aren't close to them. You can't add value if you don't know what they value. And they won't ever go the extra mile for a leader who doesn't care about them.

I learned that at age twenty-five. And that's when I made a different choice: I will open my heart to people and try to love them unconditionally. That has caused some of the greatest hurts in my life. It has also created some of my greatest joys.

So the bottom-line answer to the question about changing your heart toward people is that it is a choice. You must *decide* to love people and be authentic and vulnerable with them. You must choose to let them into your life so that you can add value to them and they can add value to you.

I believe that such a decision will lead to many more wins than losses, both personally and professionally. Once you've been part of a team in which people give not just their minds but also their hearts, you won't ever want to go back. You'll always want to be open with people.

6. If I Am Reaching Goals and Achieving Success, Why Should I Take Care of Developing Myself as a Leader?

Growth is the great separator of those who succeed long term from those who do not. As time goes by, the gap that separates those who grow intentionally and those who don't widens. If

> Growth is the great separator of those who succeed long term from those who do not.

you're young now, you may not see a gap. As you age, you will.

Warren Bennis and Burt Nanus observed, "It is the capacity to develop and improve their skills that distinguishes leaders from followers." So the short answer is that if you want to be a leader, you need to keep growing. What got you to where you are today will not get you to where you want to go tomorrow. You must grow into your tomorrows. The choice is yours whether or not you will.

I love the way Chuck Swindoll expresses this idea. He writes,

A piano sits in a room, gathering dust. It is full of the music of the masters, but in order for such strains to flow from it, fingers must strike the keys... trained fingers, representing endless hours of disciplined dedication. You do not have to practice. The piano neither requires it nor demands it. If, however, you want to draw a beautiful music from the piano, that discipline is required....

You do not have to pay the price to grow and expand intellectually. The mind neither requires it nor demands it. If, however, you want to experience the joy of discovery and the pleasure of plowing new and fertile soil, effort is required.

Light won't automatically shine upon you nor will truth silently seep into your head by means of rocking-chair osmosis.

It's up to you. It's your move.[17]

Do you want to be ready for the next opportunity when it comes? When it arrives, it will be too late to prepare. The time to get ready is now.

My friend Dan Reiland understood this. When he started working at Skyline Church in San Diego, he was in his twenties. Though Dan was dedicated to growth, he could see that many of his friends and colleagues in their twenties were not growing. He could see that it would catch up with them when they reached their thirties. If they didn't change, many would experience midlife crises in their forties and fifties. So Dan did something about it. He started a yearlong leadership and mentoring process called Joshua's Men. He has invested in leaders and helped them learn to grow for over thirty years. Literally hundreds of people have learned from him.

You don't know what life will throw at you. You will face tragedies and opportunities. How do you know you will be ready for them? Grow today.

A Plan for Growth Requires...

Growth does not just happen on its own. You have to be intentional about it. If you want to grow, plan to grow. Here are the things you'll need to do:

1. Set aside time to grow.
2. Determine your areas of growth.
3. Find resources in your areas of growth.
4. Apply what you learn daily.

---

7. How Do You Lead with Humility When in the Tough Corporate World It's Viewed as a Weakness?

I think this question reveals a misconception about the corporate world. People in business don't automatically see humility as weakness. They see weakness as weakness—weakness in preparation, skills, work ethic, etc. People who achieve at a high level of excellence can smell weakness.

That brings up the question of what humility is. Humility doesn't mean being weak. It just means thinking of yourself less. It means being realistic

> **Humility doesn't mean being weak. It just means thinking of yourself less.**

and grounded. It means valuing others and their contributions. People like working with a leader with those characteristics. I think the research of Jim Collins in *Good to Great* bears this out. Collins writes,

> Level 5 leaders are a study in duality: modest and willful, humble and fearless. To quickly grasp this concept, think of United States President Abraham Lincoln…who never let his ego get in the way of his primary ambition for the larger cause of an enduring nation. Yet those who mistook Mr. Lincoln's personal modesty… as [a sign] of weakness found themselves terribly mistaken.[18]

Pride is a weakness, but humility isn't. Pride is a roadblock to personal progress, good leadership, and positive team building. Here are a few reasons why:

PRIDE	HUMILITY
Discounts team building	Encourages team building
Makes us unteachable	Values teachability
Closes our minds to feedback	Opens us up to feedback
Prevents us from admitting mistakes	Allows us to face our mistakes
Distorts our perception of reality	Enables us to face reality
Prompts poor character choices	Promotes character building
Limits our potential	Enlarges our potential

The ancient Proverbs writer observed, "People who accept correction are on the pathway to life, but those who ignore it will lead others away."[19] If you pair excellence with humility, people not only won't run over you, they will respect you.

8. How Transparent Should a Leader Be? Is It OK for the Team to Know of Personal Challenges, Such as Cancer?

As a leader, you should not hide bad news. Intuitive people can sense that there is bad news, even if you don't disclose it. And in this era of transparency, people always find out. So it behooves leadership to be candid.

Of course, there are times to not be totally candid with people. For example, if you have a family member whose privacy needs to be protected, you need to honor that. But in general, people appreciate transparency. It allows them to connect. And it can inspire them. That was certainly the case in England during World War II. Winston Churchill didn't shirk from telling the British people how dire the odds were in May 1940, as Britain stood alone against the Nazi war machine. The people didn't panic. Their resolve increased, and they stood firm.

As you weigh whether or not to tell people bad news, the question you need to ask yourself is why you're telling it. Are you doing it for the good of the team? Are you communicating to connect with your people and to encourage them? Or are you doing it because you are hoping people will pick you up? If it's the latter, that's not a good reason. And if you're going through a personal crisis, it's OK to let people know that you may not be yourself right now, but that it'll only be for a season. Then carry on. You don't want to wear your people out with your personal challenges.

9. The Leadership Process Is a Long Journey—Lasting a Lifetime. How Can I Overcome the Loneliness I Sometimes Feel?

First of all, let me point out that there's a difference between aloneness and loneliness. I sometimes crave aloneness—to think, create, and hear from God. I've written often about my thinking chair, the place in my office where I like to take time to think and reflect. I enjoy that time. I've spoken less often about the times when I awaken in the middle of the night. When I was in my late twenties, I started waking up at three or three thirty a.m. It happened about once a week. I sensed that it was a great time for me to think, reflect, pray, and meditate, so I made a commitment that if I woke up for no apparent reason, I'd get up, grab my legal pad, and spend time quietly thinking and listening. Sometimes I'd be up for an hour or two. Sometimes all night. It's been a regular habit for me. I'd estimate that 80 percent of the ideas I've had over the years have come during those times.

Aloneness fills me up. I meet it with a sense of anticipation. Loneliness is altogether different. Leaders often have to go first. That can be lonely. There are weights that leaders need to carry. There are messages that they must be the ones to communicate. There are critical decisions they must make. In a well-led organization, 90 percent of decisions are made by the people close to the problems—at the level of implementation. The other 10 percent are tough decisions that must be made by a leader.

I find loneliness draining. On one hand, it is one of the prices you pay for leadership. But there are things you can do to help you with loneliness. The best thing is to have someone in your life who loves you unconditionally, someone who will listen and with whom you connect emotionally. That person doesn't need to be a leader or understand the complexity of your world. He or she just needs to share the journey. For me that person was my mom. I could tell her anything. When she died three years ago, it was a huge loss for me. Fortunately, there are others in my life I can talk to. When I have to make a tough decision, I share it with people in my inner circle. That helps greatly, but no one else is Mom.

> Let loneliness drive you to aloneness. When you are feeling the weight of leadership, find ways to get by yourself and think things through.

The other thing you can do is let loneliness drive you to aloneness. When you are feeling the weight of leadership, find ways to get by yourself and think things through.

10. How Can Leaders Develop the Ability to "Filter" Their Emotions to Make Good Leadership Decisions?

One of the most important principles of decision making for leaders is to not make decisions at an emotional low point. When you're in an emotional valley, your perspective isn't good. Everything looks difficult. The mountains around you look huge. You can't tell how high they are or how far you are from being able to reach a goal. In contrast, when you're on the mountaintop, you can see almost everything. You can tell how deep the valleys really are. You can tell how high up you are. And you can survey the other mountains, both large and small, around you. So whenever possible, try to make major decisions when you have good perspective.

Having said that, I acknowledge that there are times when you *must* make leadership decisions during emotionally difficult times. To help you in such circumstances, here is what I advise:

1. Do Your Homework

The first defense against having unfiltered emotions negatively affect your decision making is to consider the facts. Define the issue.

Put it in writing if needed. Then gather information, considering the credibility of your sources. The more solid information you have, the better you can fight irrational emotions.

2. List Your Options and Where They Could Lead

Another part of the fact-finding process is to think about outcomes. Brainstorm every option you can think of and what the potential results could be. This will help you root out ideas that feel good emotionally but aren't strong rationally.

3. Seek Advice from the Right People

There are two kinds of people you need to consult. The first group includes the people necessary to make a decision happen. If they aren't on board, you will be in trouble if you make the decision. The second consists of people with success in the area of consideration who have your interests at heart. They can give you good advice.

4. Listen to Your Instincts

You don't want your emotions to run away with you when you're making decisions, but you also don't want to ignore your instincts. Professor and management consultant Weston H. Agor calls intuition "what we know for sure without knowing for certain." Often your instincts warn you in a way that goes beyond the facts. Psychologist Joyce Brothers advised, "Trust your hunches. They're usually based on facts filed away just below the conscious level."

> "Intuition is what we know for sure without knowing for certain."
> —*Weston H. Agor*

Judging Your Intuitive Track Record

When do you know if listening to your intuition is a good idea? Ask yourself these questions:

Am I an intuitive leader?
Are my hunches usually right?
Do I know a lot about the area in which I am making a decision?
Do I have a lot of successful experience in this area?
Am I gifted in this area?

---

5. Make Decisions Based on Principles and Values You Believe In

When all is said and done, you must be able to live with the decisions you make. When I have to make a difficult or emotional one, I am inspired by Abraham Lincoln, who said, "I desire to conduct the affairs of this administration in such a way that if at the end, when I come to lay down the reins of power, I have lost every other friend on earth, I shall have at least one friend left and that friend shall be down inside of me."

Leading yourself is perhaps the least discussed yet most important aspect of leadership. What happens when leaders fail to do the right things internally, day in and day out? They get into trouble. The news is littered with the names of people with great talent and huge opportunities who did wrong things and cultivated bad habits when others weren't looking.

If you and I want to be successful in life, successful in leadership, and successful in finishing well, we must learn to lead ourselves successfully.

Questions Related to How Leadership Works

1. Does everyone have the potential to be an effective leader?
2. How can you be a leader right where you are, even if you're at the bottom?
3. What is the ultimate purpose of leadership?
4. What is the difference between delegating and abdicating responsibility?
5. What is the greatest challenge in answering the call to leadership?
6. Can a leader actually lead and serve at the same time?
7. What are the top skills required to lead people through sustained difficult times?
8. Is it possible to be a leader in all areas of your life?
9. What are the rhythms of leadership as you go from your twenties to your thirties to your forties and beyond? What should you develop, change, take hold of, or let go of as you grow into each season?

5

How Does Leadership Work?

When I began my career, leadership wasn't something I thought about. There were things I thought were important, such as attitude. When I was a junior in high school, my coach made me a captain because he said my attitude was good, so that became important to me. I had been taught that a strong work ethic was crucial to success, so I worked hard. I went into my first position thinking that my title made me a leader, but I quickly found out that people in the organization followed others instead of me.

In those early years, my goal was to get things done. I wanted to help people and grow the organization. I tried different things. Some worked, others didn't. Then I read J. Oswald Sanders's book *Spiritual Leadership*. In it I came across this:

> Leadership is influence, the ability of one person to influence others to follow his or her lead. Famous leaders have always known this.[20]

These words changed my life. It became clear to me why my position and title had done little to help me. I needed to become a better leader. I needed to learn how to influence people. Leadership became the focus of my personal growth.

Everything rises and falls on leadership. Armed with the knowledge that leadership was the key to building teams, growing organizations, and fulfilling visions, I set out to teach leadership. I organized my first leadership conference and—nobody came. Well, that's not *exactly* true. Seventeen people showed up, but I had hoped and planned for ten times that number. The next conference was poorly attended too. And the next. When I began talking to people about it, I discovered that people thought, "I'm already a leader. Why would I come to a leadership conference?" They believed that their positions made them leaders, just as I had. That's when I started telling everyone who would listen, "Leadership is influence." In time, people started coming to the conferences because they wanted to have more influence with others. As they developed more influence, they became more effective and so did their organizations.

Leadership is a complex subject. I'm sixty-seven years old and I'm still learning. I intend to be a student of leadership until the day I die. But I will never lose sight of the truth that leadership starts with influence and builds from there. Please keep that in mind as you read this chapter.

1. Does Everyone Have the Potential to Be an Effective Leader?

I believe what you're really asking is whether leadership is an exclusive club only for those who were born with the ability. My answer to that is no. Everyone has the potential to lead on some level, and anyone can become better at leading. While it is true that some people are born with traits that help them to become better leaders than others, those natural traits are only the beginning.

British author Leonard Ravenhill told the story of a group of tourists visiting a picturesque village where they saw an old man sitting by a fence. In a rather patronizing way, one of the visitors asked, "Were any great men born in this village?"

Without looking up the old man replied, "No, only babies."[21]

Great leaders don't start out great. Like all people they start out as babies, and grow to become adequate, then good, then great leaders. Leadership is developed, not discovered. It's a process. Three main components come into play in the development of a leader:

Environment: Incarnation of Leadership

A person's environment has a tremendous impact on him. Leadership is more caught than taught. I learned this at home as a kid because I grew up in the home of a fantastic leader: my father. Not only did he model good leadership, he also did his best to draw the best out of us. He

> **Leadership is developed, not discovered.**

identified our gifts and talents early, and encouraged us to go with our strengths in our development. And he praised and rewarded us when we demonstrated strong character and good leadership.

If you grew up in a leadership environment, you probably recognized your own leadership ability early, as I did. Your environment and the leaders who created it put leadership *in* you. It became part of you and maybe you weren't even aware that it was happening.

If you're in a positive leadership environment now, you are probably having leadership qualities encouraged in you and they may be starting to come out. The right environment always makes learning easier. Live in an artistic environment, and creativity often becomes natural to you. Live in a sporting environment, and you gravitate toward sports. Live in a leadership environment, and you become a better leader.

If you're not in a leadership environment now, and have never spent time in one, you may be having difficulty knowing what it means to lead. If so, you will need to find a positive leadership environment to help you in your leadership development. Is it possible to learn leadership without a conducive environment? Yes, but it's difficult, and your development will be slow. William Bernbach, co-founder of the advertising agency Doyle Dane Bernbach, was indicating this when he said, "I'm amused when other agencies try to hire my people away. They'd have to 'hire' the whole environment. For a flower to blossom, you need the right soil as well as the right seed."

What Does a Growth Environment Look Like?

Others are *Ahead* of me.
I am continually *Challenged*.
My focus is *Forward*.
The atmosphere is *Affirming*.
I am often out of my *Comfort Zone*.
I wake up *Excited*.
Failure is not my *Enemy*.
Others are *Growing*.
People desire *Change*.
Growth is *Modeled* and *Expected*.

Exposure: Inspiration for Leadership

One of the things I find most inspiring is exposure to great leaders. My father gets the credit for first introducing me to leaders. When I was in high school, he took me to see Norman Vincent Peale and E. Stanley Jones. He required me to read books that introduced me to leadership concepts. After I graduated from college, I continued to seek out leaders and speakers to learn from them, people like Zig

Ziglar, Elmer Towns, Peter Drucker, and John Wooden. I've learned so much from them and been inspired to pursue larger visions by them.

I love to hear great leaders speak. I get ideas from reading their books. I enjoy asking them questions. I get fired up watching them lead. I am even inspired by getting to visit their work spaces. I particularly enjoyed visiting Adolph Rupp's office at the University of Kentucky and sitting in the original locker room he coached from. I loved playing basketball as a kid, so I imagined myself as one of his players, listening to one of his fiery speeches before a game or going through his half-time adjustments before taking the court.

I've also visited every presidential library, from Washington's to Clinton's. (As I write this, the libraries of George W. Bush and Barack Obama have not yet been opened.) When Margaret and I visit a library, we spend an entire day just soaking in leadership and being inspired by it.

Where Will You Go for Leadership Inspiration?

Whom do you admire as leaders? Plan to go hear someone you admire speak. Take a trip to a presidential library or a museum. Make an appointment to interview an impactful leader. Get inspired!

Equipping: Intention for Leadership

Leadership is influence, and for that reason it can be taught. You can learn to connect with people. You can learn how to communicate. You can learn to plan and strategize. You can learn to prioritize. You can learn how to get people to work together. You can learn how to train and equip people. You can learn to inspire and motivate others. Most leadership skills can be taught to people; people can be equipped to lead.

This is the reason I've spent the last thirty years of my life focused on writing books and developing resources to help people grow and learn. I believe every person can be equipped to lead. I find it highly rewarding when people let me know that I have helped them in some way to grow as leaders.

Recently I received an e-mail from J. M. Hardy in which he said,

> Tonight I write to give you thanks for the impact you have made on my life. I have collected hundreds of your tapes and every book or CD that you ever produced. Through your long distance mentoring I have overcome the challenges of my youth. Today I have things many others only dream of. I have a bachelors and masters degree in leadership studies. I am now preparing for my Ph.D. I work for a *Fortune* 100 company where I am responsible for over $120 million in sales and 500 employees. I have a beautiful wife and three children in college.
>
> From my family to yours, God bless you and thank you. I will be waiting for your next lesson and the next book you write. I can never say thank you enough. I will most likely never meet you or get to shake your hand, but I want you to know how much I appreciate you and all you have done, even when you didn't know you were doing it.

When I read a message like that, I could teach and write for another thirty years!

The one thing you can do to have the greatest impact on your leadership potential is to be intentional every day about becoming equipped to lead. Every book you read, every lesson you absorb, every principle you apply helps you to become a better leader and takes you another step forward in your leadership potential.

> **The one thing you can do to have the greatest impact on your leadership potential is to be intentional every day about becoming equipped to lead.**

What Is Your Plan for Leadership Growth?

If you do not have a plan, the odds are against your growing as a leader. Set some goals and develop a personal strategy to grow in the coming year. Then break down the plan into daily and weekly disciplines.

---

2. How Can You Be a Leader Right Where You Are, Even if You're at the Bottom?

The good news is that you can be a leader no matter where you are. You don't need a title. You don't need a position. You don't need a formal education. All you need to begin is the desire to lead and the willingness to learn. The key is influence.

Leadership Is Influence

As I've already discussed, leadership starts with influence. Your ability to influence others will be the single greatest factor in your success as a leader. Author and professor Harry Allen Overstreet asserted, "The very essence of all power to influence lies in getting the other person to participate." Influence is an invitation anyone can make to another person.

I love the leader's prayer written by Pauline H. Peters: "God, when I am wrong, make me willing to change. When I am right, make me easy to live with. So strengthen me that the power of my example will far exceed the authority of my rank."

Influencing Others Is a Choice

Recently I had dinner with Jim Collins, author of *Good to Great*. We talked about many things, including leadership. One of the things

Jim told me was, "You're not the first person to say that leadership is influence, but you have proven it to be true."

At the beginning of this chapter, I told you the story of why I started telling people that leadership is influence. The reality is that influence is a choice. We can be indifferent to people, pursue our own agendas, have bad attitudes, and refuse to work with a team. Or we can care about people, be inclusive, work to be positive, cooperate with others, and try to positively influence them. Every day it is our choice. If we choose to try to influence people, we can lead from anywhere.

Our Influence Is Not Equal in All Areas

Just because you have influence with someone doesn't mean you have influence with everyone. Influence must develop with each individual. If you don't believe me, try ordering around someone else's dog! I once came upon a poem called "A Born Leader" that describes this well:

I'm paid to be a foreman.
My job is leading men.
My boss thinks I'm a natural,
But if I am, why then,
I wish someone would tell me
Why snow-swept walks I clean,
When in the house sit two grown sons
Who made the football team.[22]

I discuss the process of developing influence with others in *The 5 Levels of Leadership*. In summary, it starts with *Position*, grows to *Permission* as you develop a relationship, builds upon *Production* as you help others get things done, strengthens as you engage in

People Development, and culminates at the *Pinnacle* when you raise up other leaders who develop people. The most effective leaders are intentional about trying to positively influence others. And they understand that they have to work to increase their influence with individual people.

With Influence Comes Responsibility

In our culture, people tend to focus on their rights. Because much of the history of humanity is the story of leaders trampling those they lead, the founders of the United States had a strong conviction that they should protect certain inalienable rights with which people are endowed by their creator. That has led to unprecedented freedom in our nation, which is an extraordinary thing. Unfortunately it has overemphasized rights to our culture's detriment.

People who desire to lead often seek leadership positions because of the perks and privileges. However, as leaders we should always be aware that leadership carries responsibility, that what we do affects the people whose feelings and well-being are within our influence. The influence we have with others will be positive or negative. We choose which one it will be.

People of Positive Influence Add Value to Others

Groundbreaking Major League Baseball player Jackie Robinson observed, "A life isn't significant except for its impact upon other lives." If you choose to influence others and become a better leader, I hope you will do so to add value to others.

> **"A life isn't significant except for its impact upon other lives."**
> —*Jackie Robinson*

3. What Is the Ultimate Purpose of Leadership?

First and foremost, leadership is about adding value to people. Author Norman Vincent Peale said, "To be successful is to be helpful, caring, and constructive, to make everything and everyone you touch a little bit better. The best thing you have to give is yourself." If you want to be successful as a leader, you need to make others better. You need to help them remove self-imposed limitations and encourage them to reach their potential. You can do that by doing the following:

Listen to Their Story and Ask Questions

You don't really understand people until you hear their life story. If you know their stories, you grasp their history, their hurts, their hopes and aspirations. You put yourself in their shoes. And just by virtue of listening and remembering what's important to them, you communicate that you care and desire to add value.

Make Their Agendas Your Priority

Too many leaders think that leadership is all about themselves. Good leaders focus on the needs and wants of their people, and as far as it is within their power, they make their people's hopes and dreams a priority. There is great power when the vision of the organization and the dreams of its people come into alignment, and everybody wins.

Believe in Them

If you want to help people, believe in them. When people believe in themselves, they perform better. That's why I say it's wonderful when the people believe in the leader; it's more wonderful when the leader believes in the people.

How do you increase people's belief in themselves? You express your belief in them. In general, people rise to the level of your expectations. I call this putting a "10" on people's heads, meaning that you see everyone as a winner or potential winner. If you see the value in everyone and let them know that you value them, it helps them, it helps the organization, and it helps you as a leader.

Discuss Ways to Accomplish Their Visions and Create Plans that Fit Them

When you know what makes people tick and you understand their hopes and dreams, you have the potential to add value to them in a powerful way. Talk to them about ways to help them accomplish their vision while they do their work and help the organization. Then, together, formulate a plan to help them do it.

Help Them Until the Vision Is Accomplished

It's one thing to say you want to help people on your team. It's another to actually follow through and assist them all along the way. When you follow through, you not only help them, you also build your leadership credibility and your influence, not only with them, but with everyone on the team.

There is no downside to adding value to people. Yes, it will cost you time and effort. But when you add value to people, you help them and make them more valuable. If you're a leader, when your people are on purpose and content, you help your team. When your team is more effective, you help your organization

> There is no downside to adding value to people.

because it becomes better. And the whole process will bring you a deep sense of satisfaction.

4. What Is the Difference Between Delegating and Abdicating Responsibility?

When leaders hand off tasks to others, they typically do it in one of two ways: they delegate tasks or they dump them. Author Roger Fritz asserted, "Dumping is indiscriminate. It's done for expedience, taking no account of the strengths and weaknesses of the person who is supposed to do the work."

People who abdicate responsibility neglect leadership when they dump tasks on other people. Good leaders always take into account the skills, abilities, and interests of the person doing the work. Dumping usually happens on the spur of the moment. It ignores the person's need for more information or training. Dumping often occurs when people in authority want to get rid of a problem or remove an unpleasant task from their plate.

In contrast, good delegation includes carefully selecting the right person for a task. Good leaders take into account the skills and abilities best suited to complete the task at hand. Leaders who delegate well establish what the goals are, grant the authority to get the job done, and supply the necessary resources for the job, yet encourage independent action on the part of the person doing the work. They buy into the philosophy expressed by General George S. Patton, who said, "Never tell people how to do things. Tell them what to do and they will surprise you with their ingenuity."

In the end the leader who delegates the job is still responsible for seeing that the job gets done. Byron Dorgan observed, "You can delegate authority, but you cannot delegate responsibility." If the task doesn't get done, if you're the leader, the buck stops with you.

5. What Is the Greatest Challenge in Answering the Call to Leadership?

The greatest challenge in leadership is making decisions that affect other people. It's hard to make good decisions every day for people. That's why some leaders would rather act like the French revolutionary who said, "There go my people. I must find out where they're going, so I can lead them."

> The greatest challenge in leadership is making decisions that affect other people.

The loneliest place in leadership is reserved for the person who makes the first decision. What leaders do and why they do it are often misunderstood. But the fact that decision making can be difficult and painful doesn't let leaders off of the hook. They still need to make early and tough decisions, because leaders who decline to make decisions create insecurity among followers and undermine their own leadership.

If you want to become a better leader, become willing to make tough choices and uncomfortable decisions. Those may include the following:

Courageous Decisions: What Must Be Done

Peter Drucker, who has been called the father of modern management, observed, "Whenever you see a successful business, someone once made a courageous decision." Hard-won progress often comes as the result of difficult decisions that can be scary. Sometimes the organization is on the line and the only people in a position to make the courageous calls are the leaders.

Priority Decisions: What Must Be Done First

It is the responsibility of leaders to look ahead, see the bigger picture, understand the greater vision, and make decisions based on the priorities of the whole team and organization. Italian economist Vil-fredo Pareto said, "If you're Noah, and your ark is about to sink, look for the elephants first, because you can throw over a bunch of cats and dogs and squirrels and everything else that is just a small animal—and your ark will keep sinking. But if you can find one elephant to get overboard, you're in much better shape."

Change Decisions: What Must Be Done Differently

One of the most difficult yet vital roles of leaders is to be change agents for the sake of the team and organization. Most people don't like change. They fear it and resist it. Jim Rohn asserted, "If someone is going down the wrong road, he doesn't need motivation to speed him up. What he needs is education to turn him around." Leaders often provide the education and impetus for making changes.

Creative Decisions: What Might Be Possible

Someone once said that 95 percent of the decisions leaders make can be made by a reasonably intelligent high school sophomore. Leaders get paid for the other 5 percent. Sometimes making those tough decisions calls for experience. But often what's really beneficial is cre-ativity. Good leaders think outside the box and help the team break through barriers and cover new ground.

People Decisions: Who Should—and Should Not—Be Involved

The most difficult of all decisions often directly involve people. It's not always easy to find the right person for a given job. It's even more difficult to decide whether someone is no longer right for the team. In fact, this is such an important and complex process that I've dedicated an entire chapter to resolving conflict and leading challenging people.

Though decision making is difficult, it is vital to good leadership. H. W. Andrews asserted, "Failure to make a decision after due consideration of all the facts will quickly brand a man as unfit for a position of responsibility. Not all of your decisions will be correct. None of us is perfect. But if you get into the habit of making decisions, experience will develop your judgment to a point where more and more of your decisions will be right." And as a result, you will become a better leader.

6. Can a Leader Actually Lead and Serve at the Same Time?

It is a common misconception that it's the role of followers to serve and of leaders to be served. That is a faulty view of good leadership. When Ed Zore, chairman and former CEO of Northwestern Mutual, was working his way up in the company, he thought that when he reached the top, he would be in complete control of his life and organization—the captain of his own ship, someone who could do whatever he wanted. What he discovered was that leadership is actually servanthood.

Most potential leaders overestimate the perks and underestimate the price of leadership. When they focus on the benefits of leadership, they become self-serving. Here's the difference between the two kinds of leaders:

Self-serving leaders ask, "What are others doing for me?"
Serving leaders ask, "What am I doing for others?"
Self-serving leaders see people as workers they own.
Serving leaders see people as teammates on loan.

Self-serving leaders put their own interests ahead of the team's.
Serving leaders put the team's interests ahead of their own.
Self-serving leaders manipulate people to their own advantage.
Serving leaders motivate people for mutual advantage.

If you want to be the best leader you can possibly be, no matter how much or how little natural leadership talent you possess, you need to become a serving leader. And here's the good news: it's a choice. What it takes to serve others is within your control:

1. Serving Others Is an Attitude Issue

Leon A. Gorman of L.L. Bean observed, "Service is just a day-in, day-out, ongoing, never-ending, unremitting, persevering, compassionate type of activity." First and foremost, it's a matter of attitude. And it's contagious.

I have been blessed for over twenty-five years by the fantastic attitude of one of my team members: Linda Eggers. She has a heart to serve, and when others see her serving, it makes them want to serve. Linda says, "One of the greatest gifts God has given me is the opportunity to work as John's assistant. Since one of my gifts is service, doing tasks for him is relatively easy. So I am always looking for ways to go the extra mile and do more than what is expected for him, his family, and for the people I interface with on his behalf. I have a 'whatever it takes and whenever he needs it' mentality knowing that I share in his ministry behind the scenes."

I am a better person because Linda serves me so well, and it motivates me to serve her and the other people on my team.

2. Serving Others Is a Motives Issue

Robert K. Greenleaf, founder of the Robert K. Greenleaf Center for Servant Leadership, observed, "The servant-leader *is* servant first. . . .

It begins with the natural feeling that one wants to serve, to serve *first*. Then conscious choice brings one to aspire to lead.... The difference manifests itself in the care taken by the servant-first to make sure that other people's highest priority needs are served." If you go into leadership with the motive to serve others, the team, and the organization, it will be hard for you to go wrong.

3. Serving Others Is a Values Issue

If you value people, you will want to add value to them and serve them. I know that may sound idealistic to some leaders. However, there is also a very pragmatic value to serving others. Everything you will accomplish as a leader ultimately hinges on the people you work with. Without them your success as a leader will be greatly limited. Every day, organizations are responsible for the greatest waste in business—that of human potential. If you can develop people and help them discover their strength zones, everybody wins.

> If you value people, you will want to add value to them and serve them.

I believe there is no division between serving and leading. The foundation of effective leadership is actually service. On a personal level, I can't imagine serving without leadership, and can't imagine leadership without serving. And people can tell what your attitude is. It shows in everything you do. For example, whenever one of my organizations puts on an event, I tell them not to create a head table. Most big functions put all the dignitaries together at a table in the front of the room. It creates a separation between them and everyone else. That's not the right attitude for a serving leader, and it sends a negative message.

Good leaders serve. They see their role as that of servant, facilitator, value adder, success-bringer—but they do this quietly, without fanfare. Their mind-set is like that described by tennis star Arthur

Ashe, who said, "True heroism is remarkably sober, very undramatic. It is not the urge to surpass all others at whatever cost, but the urge to serve others at whatever cost."

Questions Leaders Should Ask About Serving

Are you a serving leader? To find out, ask yourself these questions:

1. Why do I want to lead others?
2. How important is status to me?
3. Do others work *for* me or *with* me?
4. Am I glad to serve others and do it cheerfully?
5. Is my team better because I am on it?
6. Exactly how is it better?

If you find it difficult or "beneath" you to serve others, your heart may not be right. To earn the right to lead in greater things, first learn to serve in smaller ones.

---

7. What Are the Top Skills Required to Lead People Through Sustained Difficult Times?

One of the most challenging tasks any leader faces is being a change agent and leading people through tough times. But it can also be one of the most rewarding. Economist John Kenneth Galbraith asserted, "All of the great leaders have had one characteristic in common: it was the willingness to confront unequivocally the major anxiety of their people in their time."

Tough times show us ourselves. The people we lead find out who they are. As leaders, we also find out what we're made of. As author

Jack Kinder says, "You're not made in a crisis—you're revealed. When you squeeze an orange—you get orange juice. When you squeeze a lemon—you get lemon juice. When a human being gets squeezed— you get what is inside—positive or negative."

The best way to approach tough times is to try to see them as opportunities. Most people want their problems to be fixed without their having to face them, but that is an impossibility. As a leader, as a coach, as a catalyst for turnaround, you need to help people solve problems, take responsibility, and work to make things better. Most of the time, people need to dig themselves out of their difficulties—whether or not they were the cause of them. They need help, which you can give them in the form of advice, encouragement, and positive reinforcement, but everyone needs to do his or her part and work together.

With that context in mind, here is how I would recommend that you lead and serve people during difficult times:

1. Define Reality

Most people's reaction to tough times or a crisis is to say, "Let's forget the whole thing." Maybe that's why Peter Drucker said, "A time of turbulence is a dangerous time, but its greatest danger is a temptation to deny reality." So what is a leader to do? Define reality for people. That's what Max De Pree advised. He said it was a leader's first responsibility.

The Law of the Scoreboard in my book *The 17 Indisputable Laws of Teamwork* says the team can make adjustments when it knows where it stands. As the leader of a team, you need to help people define the things that are holding them back. Then you need to define the things that will free them up. People cannot make good choices if they don't know what these things are, and many have a hard time figuring them out on their own. You're there to help them.

2. Remind Them of the Big Picture

Winifred E. Newman, associate professor in the Architecture Department of Florida International University, observed, "Vision is the world's most desperate need. There are no hopeless situations, only people who think hopelessly." Leaders are keepers and communicators of the vision. They bear the responsibility for always seeing the big picture and helping their people to see it. People need to be reminded of why they are doing what they do, and of the benefits that await them as a reward for their hard work.

That doesn't mean that the vision is 100 percent clear to the leader, especially during difficult times. But that's OK. Author and friend Andy Stanley says, "Uncertainty is not an indication of poor leadership; it underscores the need for leadership.... The nature of leadership demands that there always be an element of uncertainty. The temptation is to think, 'If I were a good leader, I would know exactly what to do.' Increased responsibility means dealing more with more intangibles and therefore more complex uncertainty. Leaders can afford to be uncertain, but we cannot afford to be unclear. People will not follow fuzzy leadership."

When I'm leading people through a difficult situation, I often don't know all the answers. But I know there *are* answers, and I will do everything I can to make sure we find out what they are. That gives people reassurance.

3. Help Them Develop a Plan

Before you can develop a strategy to get out of a difficult situation, you must know where you are and where you want to go. If you have helped people by defining reality and showing them the big picture, the next task is to identify the steps required to go from here to there. Not everyone finds it easy to do that. As a leader, you need to come alongside them and help them figure it out.

4. Help Them Make Good Choices

One of my favorite sayings is, "There is a choice you have to make in everything you do. So keep in mind that in the end, the choice you make, makes you."[23] People's choices define who they are and determine where they go. It's true that we don't choose everything we get in life, but much of what we get comes from what we've chosen.

As a leader, the more good choices you have made throughout your life, the better you have probably positioned yourself to help others, not only because you have gained experience and developed wisdom, but also because repeated good choices often lead to personal success and greater options. If these things are true for you, put them to good use by helping others navigate difficult waters.

5. Value and Promote Teamwork

Two shipwrecked men in tattered clothes slouch together at one end of a lifeboat. They watch casually as three people at the other end of the boat bail furiously, trying to keep the vessel afloat. One man then says to the other, "Thank God that hole isn't in our end of the boat!" When times get tough, everybody needs to work together if they want to get the team out of trouble.

The Law of Mount Everest in *The 17 Indisputable Laws of Teamwork* states, "As the challenge escalates, the need for teamwork elevates." No team can win and keep winning unless everyone works together. It's the responsibility of leaders to promote teamwork and get team members cooperating and working together.

6. Give Them Hope

John W. Gardner, former secretary of health, education, and welfare, said, "The first and last task of a leader is to keep hope alive—the hope that we can finally find our way through to a better world—despite the day's action, despite our own inertness and shallowness and wavering resolve." Hope is the foundation of change. If we continue to hold hope high, and we help others to do the same, there is always a chance to move forward and succeed.

Crisis holds the opportunity to be reborn. Difficult times can discipline us to become stronger. Conflict can actually renew our chances of building better relationships. It's not always easy to remember these things. As leaders, our job is to remind people of the possibilities and to help them succeed.

8. Is It Possible to Be a Leader in All Areas of Your Life?

The short answer to this question is no. And here's why. You cannot develop influence with everyone. There isn't enough time in a day or enough days in a year. Developing influence is a process. I describe this in *The 5 Levels of Leadership*. People start their influence journey at Level 1: Position. You don't have to hold a position or title to start developing influence with others, but if you do have a position, you must recognize that it's only a starting point.

To begin to truly influence people, you must develop relationships. This is accomplished on Level 2: Permission. To build upon that and gain more influence, you must help people to be effective and work together with others on a team. This occurs on Level 3: Production. All these things take time. You cannot develop deep enough relationships in every area of your life. You cannot help everyone you know to be productive. It's impossible.

So what do you do? Choose where you will invest yourself to develop influence and become an effective leader. The leadership skills you develop will help you in all areas of life, but you cannot expect to lead in every area of life. That simply isn't realistic.

9. What Are the Rhythms of Leadership as You Go from Your Twenties to Your Thirties to Your Forties and Beyond? What Should You Develop, Change, Take Hold of, or Let Go of as You Grow into Each Season?

The decades of life are not the same for everyone. We all know that. And there are both positives and negatives to every age. For example, when we're young, we have tremendous energy, but we don't know what to do with it; when we're old, we know what to do, but our bodies wear out and our energy starts to flag.

You can look at the decades of a leader's life and make some generalizations about them:

- **Twenties—Alignment:** We build our foundation and prepare for future success.
- **Thirties—Adjustment:** We try different things and find out what works and what doesn't.
- **Forties—Advancement:** We focus on our strength zone and make the most of what works.
- **Fifties—Assessment:** We reevaluate our priorities and hopefully shift from success to significance.
- **Sixties—Ascendance:** We reach the top of our game and the height of our influence.

Of course, not everyone's life works out this way. That's why I think it's more useful to think of our lives in terms of seasons. I learned about seasons in my first leadership position, in rural Indiana. Most of the people I led were farmers, and everything they did related to the seasons of the year. As leaders, we have seasons that aren't equal in length, unlike farmers. And we usually experience only one cycle in our lifetime, not cycles continually repeated annually. But we can still learn a lot from some of the truths farmers understand.

For example, every season has a beginning and an end. Our lives are not static. Even if a person chooses not to grow, life does not remain the same. (People who refuse to grow professionally, decline.) While we are in a season of life, we should do all we can. Too often people give less than their best, thinking they can make it up later. What they don't understand is that once a season has ended, they often *can't* go back. They don't get another chance. When the new season comes, we need to be ready to make the appropriate changes to move on to it.

Another truth is that the seasons always come in sequence. Spring always follows winter. Autumn always comes after summer. We have no control over the order in which the earth's seasons occur. The same is true of the seasons of success. You cannot harvest life's rewards without first planting seeds. Yet many people want to spend their entire lives in the harvest season. It just doesn't happen.

Each of us is responsible for managing the seasons of our own lives. We have all been given seeds. We all have to weather storms and drought. And it's up to us to plant and cultivate several "crops" for life simultaneously. Farmers know that beans, potatoes, tomatoes, corn, and cotton can be grown side by side. Yet they are harvested at different times. Likewise, we must recognize that we may be in one season of family life, a different season of spiritual life, and yet another of leadership life. We must do what's right for the season in each area, and do things in order, if we want to eventually see harvests in life.

Ecclesiastes says, "There is a time for everything, and a season for every activity under the heavens."[24] Many people fail because they are out of sync with time and place in their seasons of life. Sometimes their failure has nothing to do with determination or willingness, but comes from their efforts being out of proper sequence. When this happens they become frustrated and may begin to believe that it's impossible for them to achieve anything significant, and that leads to discouragement. I believe it is possible for all people to reap a rewarding harvest according to their ability, but they must learn the secret to mastering each of the four seasons:

Winter Is the Season for Planning

To people who don't understand success and the seasons of life, winter is a bleak time. The ground is cold. The earth is unproductive. The trees are bare and seem lifeless. For unsuccessful people winter is a time of hibernation, drudgery, and low expectations.

For successful people winter is a time of beginnings. This is the time for vision and dreams. It is a time of anticipation. Goals are set and plans are made during winter, and without them, the chance of a successful harvest is slim.

Identify Your "Crops" and Their Seasons

Which areas of life are important to you? These are the fields where you plant the "crops" for your life. Have you already identified them? If not, make a list.

Once you have identified the areas of life that are important to you, determine which season you are in for each. This will help you to work your way through each of the seasons. Remember, you will not be in the same season in every area.

In any individual area of life where you're experiencing a winter, spend some time thinking about the harvest you hope to someday reap. Winter is the season of dreaming and details. You must think big and plan little. Think big about what could be. Then plan how you will get there. (If you're not sure how to go through that process, you may want to look at my book *Put Your Dream to the Test*.)

Spring Is the Season for Planting

People who don't understand the seasons of life get spring fever. They continue to daydream when they need to be working. Successful people have spring fervor. They understand that spring is the time to take winter plans and ideas and put them into action. It's a time for enthusiastic activity—getting the seeds, preparing the soil, and planting. It takes energy. It takes perseverance. It takes sacrifice. And it takes good timing.

Anyone who has planted a garden knows that you want the plants to sprout as soon as possible after the last frost date. That ensures the longest growing season and the biggest harvest. Sometimes that means sacrificing sleep to make it happen. Is it possible to plant later? Of course. But the longer you wait, the more it will reduce the harvest.

In the leadership realm, this is why people who get a head start in life are sometimes able to make such a great impact. People like Bill Gates started their planning season as teenagers, and were planting early. So if you've missed opportunities to plant in the past, don't keep waiting. Start moving! The sooner you plow and plant, the better your chance to see a good harvest.

Summer Is the Season for Perspiration

When you mention summer to most people, they think of vacation. It's the time when children are out of school, and adults try to take time off. That's not true for a farmer, nor is it for a successful person. To them summer is the time for cultivation. If you neglect in summer what you planted in spring, you will see no harvest in autumn. For the

successful person, summer is the time for continual and regular cultivation, watering, and fertilization. It is a time of great growth.

What does summer mean for someone who's not growing food for
a living? It means following through on your personal growth plan.
In winter many people dream of success. Some realize that they must
learn and grow to achieve their goals and live their dreams. Those
people plant in spring by taking a tangible step toward growth: buying
a book, subscribing to certain podcasts, finding a mentor, identifying
a conference that will help them. But for many people, the effort stops
there. They don't read the book. They stop taking time to listen to the
podcasts. They don't follow through with the advice of their mentor.
They don't attend the conference, or they do but don't apply what they
learn. They stop sweating through the hard, tedious, sometimes painful, but always productive work that summer requires.

Good leaders cultivate themselves through personal growth. They
also cultivate relationships and grow teams. That too can be slow and
difficult work. It usually takes longer than we expect and it's harder
than we hope. But there is no such thing as solitary success. Nothing
of significance was ever achieved without people working together.

Summer can be a taxing season. The days are long and there's
more work that needs to be done than there are hours in the day. But
successful people keep at it. They put in the effort—even though they
can't really see that it's paying off. And that's how it often is when
you're cultivating. You just have to keep working and trust that the
plans you made in winter and the hard work you're doing now are
going to pay off if you stick with them.

Autumn Is the Season for Produce

To people who haven't understood the seasons and who neglected
to plan in winter, plant in spring, and perspire in summer, autumn
brings regret. Just as watching trees lose their leaves can bring some

people feelings of loss, some people realize only when it's too late that they should have made hay while the sun shone. However, to successful people who have made the most of each season, autumn is a time of reaping. It is the time when they receive the products of their labor. It brings feelings of accomplishment. There is no better season of life.

Your ultimate goal as a leader should be to work hard enough and strategically enough that you have more than enough to give and share with others. As I approach age seventy, I understand this in a way I never have before. I believe God gave me a head start in life. I started early and I've spent my life planning, planting, and perspiring. And now I'm reaping in ways I never expected. I have influence beyond anything I deserve or ever imagined having, and in the time I have left on this earth, my goal is to pour out every bit of it to add value to leaders who multiply value in others. My hope is that by the day I die, I'll have been able to give away everything I've been given.

> Your ultimate goal as a leader should be to work hard enough and strategically enough that you have more than enough to give and share with others.

Maybe you didn't get to start as early as I did. That doesn't matter. Wherever you find yourself, do what's right for the season. Give it all you've got, and don't worry too much about the outcome. In time, if you understand the seasons and work with them, the harvest will come.

Questions Related to Getting Started in Leadership

1. How can a young leader establish his vision and get buy-in when he doesn't yet have a track record of success?

2. How do you determine your leadership potential?

3. How can I discover my unique purpose as a leader?

4. It is said that to be a good leader you must first be a good follower. Does this maxim hold true at all times? If so, at what point does a follower become a leader?

5. I'm a bit introverted, and I believe that being more outgoing could help me to be a leader. How can I accept my personality, yet blossom in connecting with others?

6. What advice would you give to an aspiring leader trying to take the first steps into leadership?

7. What's the first thing a leader should do when brought in from the outside to be responsible for a group or department?

8. How do you find balance between leading others and producing?

9. I'm always worried about hurting people's feelings or worried about what they will think of me. What can I do to overcome this and become a strong leader?

10. How does an emerging leader establish leadership confidence without affirmation?

6

How Do I Get Started in Leadership?

Some people have a clear vision for leadership. There is an organization they desire to create or a task they want to accomplish. They see something and they try to seize it. They start performing a service or creating a product, and if it's successful, they soon need help. When they hire their first employee, they start leading.

However, most people move into leadership differently. They find themselves in a situation where someone asks them to lead something—at work, in their community, or at church—and they agree to take on the responsibility. Or they help to give direction to a project or task because no one else is doing it, or because the person in charge is doing it so poorly that they worry it will fail. So they take charge and organize it themselves, hoping to see it succeed.

How you come into a leadership role matters less than how you handle it. And the key question you need to ask yourself is, "Why do I want to lead?" I ask that question of any person who says he wants to get into leadership. If you want to help other people, your team, and your organization, you're starting on the right foot. If your desire is to fulfill a worthy vision, one that will help people and make the world a better place, you're headed in the right direction. If you're doing it to add value to others and not just yourself, you are seeking to be a leader for the right reason. And it is your duty to become the best leader you can possibly be.

1. How Can a Young Leader Establish His Vision and Get Buy-in When He Doesn't Yet Have a Track Record of Success?

I've known a lot of young leaders who are very eager to share their vision and want to know why everyone doesn't immediately jump in to help them accomplish it. In fact, I was one of those leaders when I started out. I came to my first position with big dreams and zero experience. I wanted people to instantly follow me and fulfill the vision. I often asked myself, "Why aren't people buying in?" Instead I should have been asking, "How can I build credibility?"

Until you have credibility, don't even try to get buy-in for your vision. You won't get it. You need to earn trust before people will buy in, and you must earn it through character and competence.

When you take on a new leadership position, how much temporary trust you receive will depend on many things. The culture of the organization. The credibility of your predecessor. The influence of the people who put you into place. If the environment and the culture are negative, people may assume that you won't be a good leader and give you very little grace. In a more positive environment, people may be open to you and willing to give you the benefit of the doubt for as long as six months. During that time, what you say will hold more weight than who you are. But everyone will be watching to see if what you say and what you do line up. If you have demonstrated character and competence, your credibility will keep gaining more weight until who you are eventually has greater influence than what you say.

As people's trust grows, so will your influence. And as Stephen M.R. Covey observed, "The beauty of trust is that it erases worry and frees you to get on with other matters. Trust means confidence." It also means buy-in.

> "The beauty of trust is that it erases worry and frees you to get on with other matters. Trust means confidence."
> —Stephen M.R. Covey

To demonstrate competence as you start in leadership, begin with the basics:

- **Work hard:** There is no substitute for a good work ethic. People respect someone who works hard.
- **Think ahead:** Because your decisions affect your team, beginning with the end in mind and identifying priorities are doubly important.
- **Demonstrate excellence:** The better you are at your job, the higher your initial credibility.
- **Follow through:** Good leaders bring things to completion.

To communicate character to team members in a short time, do the following:

- **Care about the people you lead:** Any time new leaders arrive on the scene, the people on the team ask three things: Do they care for me? Can they help me? Can I trust them? If you care about people and show it, they will be able to see your good character.
- **Make things right:** Because new leaders want to impress their people, they sometimes try to hide their mistakes. That is the opposite of what they should do. When decisions don't turn out the way they were intended to, leaders owe their followers an explanation and an apology. That may feel painful in the moment, but it will develop character credibility. If they can also make amends for the mistake, that will be even better.

- **Tell the truth:** When there is consistency between the words and actions of leaders, followers know that leaders can be trusted. Honesty adds integrity to the vision and credibility to the vision caster. In the long run, people appreciate truth—even hard truth.

If you put in the slow hard work of developing credibility through character and competence, you will begin to earn trust. The more trust you gain, the more potential influence you'll have. When the team wins, you gain further credibility. When you make a mistake or the team fails, it costs. Your goal is to earn so much credibility that people buy into your leadership and never lose faith in you, because if they do you've lost credibility with the organization.

2. How Do You Determine Your Leadership Potential?

I believe that nearly everyone has the potential to lead. Maybe not everyone can become a great leader, but everyone can become a better leader. Knowing that may be encouraging, but it may not be very helpful in determining how to pursue your leadership potential.

What are the signs that you have leadership potential, that you should try to lead others starting now? You need to examine four areas to get a sense of whether it is time for you to step up and lead:

1. Pay Attention to the Need You See

Leadership begins with a need, not when someone wants to fill an empty leadership position. Sometimes people see a need and it sparks something within them, a passion. That was true for me when I began to realize that organizations floundered when they didn't have good leaders. It helped me to understand that everything rises and falls on leadership. And it made me want to do something about it.

There are many needs in this world. Are there some that strike a chord in you? If you see a need that you feel a strong desire to address, and it moves you to action, that is a sign that you have the potential to lead in that area.

2. Use Your Natural Abilities to Help Others

When the desire to address a need intersects with an ability to do something about it, sparks begin to fly. When the ability of the leader perfectly fits the need of the moment, the results can be extraordinary. Henry Ford's ability to build cars at a moment in history when they could be mass-produced changed the United States and then the world. He saw the need, he had the ability, and he took action.

You have gifts, talents, and skills that you can use to help people. It is your responsibility to learn what those abilities are and develop them. If you're not sure what they are, ask others who know you well. In addition, look at the areas where you are naturally intuitive, productive, satisfied, and influential. We tend to lead naturally in areas where we are gifted. We also add the most value when we work in those areas. Once you've discovered and developed your abilities, put them to use to help your team.

3. Make the Most of Your Passion

When you begin helping others in an area that you believe is important, you may find the passion rising in you. That's a positive sign. Passion in a leader is compelling to others. People want to follow passionate leaders. It makes them want to jump on board and join them.

General Douglas MacArthur said, "Youth is not entirely a time of life; it is a state of mind. Nobody grows old by merely living a number of years. People grow old by deserting their ideals.... You are as young as your faith, as old as your doubt; as young as your self-confidence, as old as your fear; as young as your hope, as old as your despair."

If you are new to leadership, tap into your passion and fuel it. If you're not new to leadership, make sure you don't lose your passion. A cold leader never inspired anyone to a cause. A red-hot leader inspires nearly everyone.

4. Develop Your Influence

The bottom line on leadership is that it's influence. If you want to lead, you must persuade people to work with you. People who think they're leading but have no one following them are only taking a walk.

Author and professor Harry Allen Overstreet remarked, "The person who can capture and hold attention is the person who can effectively influence human behavior. Who is a failure in life? Obviously, it is the person without influence; one to whom no one attends: the inventor who can persuade no one of the value of his device; the merchant who cannot attract enough customers into his store; the teacher whose pupils whistle or stamp or play tricks while he tries to capture their attention; the poet who writes reams of verse which no one will accept." If you want to make an impact in the world, you must be able to influence people.

If you focus your attention on a need that speaks to your heart, make the most of your abilities, tap into your passion, and develop influence, you can become a leader. And you will be able to make a difference in the world.

3. How Can I Discover My Unique Purpose as a Leader?

Martin Luther King Jr. asserted, "If a man hasn't discovered something he will die for, he isn't fit to live." I think all people desire to find the thing for which they would die, because that points them to their purpose. And I think everyone has the potential to discover it.

That's especially important for leaders, because their purpose affects the lives of not only themselves, but also other people.

> "If a man hasn't discovered something he will die for, he isn't fit to live."
> —*Martin Luther King Jr.*

But discovering your purpose takes time. First you need to know yourself. Your unique purpose must be built on your strengths. Discover your strengths and you have the opportunity to discover your purpose. Don't learn what they are, and you have very little chance of living out your purpose.

How do you get to know yourself? You can learn a lot from self-evaluation tools, such as StrengthsFinder, but some things you will learn only through trial and error. The pattern in my life has been move forward, crash, reflect, evaluate, change, move forward. As I said, this can take some time, so you must be patient. Every success and every failure can bring you another step closer to knowledge of yourself.

Once you discover your strengths, you must intentionally increase your time using them. That's when you will likely begin seeing themes emerge in your life. Life coach SuEllen Williams suggests writing out your life story in five-year increments, noting life-altering events and influential people to discover themes in your life. "If you look at what's been important to you in the past," she says, "you may start to see a theme for your life and where you've gotten off track. Once you get back on, things will start falling into place."

Your goals are to sharpen your skills and to increasingly target your work toward your strengths until you home in on the thing that makes you say, "I was born to do this." That's what Martin Luther King Jr. was talking about when he said, "If a man is called to be a street sweeper, he should sweep streets even as Michelangelo painted or Beethoven composed music or Shakespeare wrote poetry. He should sweep streets so well that all the hosts of heaven and earth will pause to say, 'Here lived a great street sweeper who did his job well.'"

What Really Matters to You?

If you're having a difficult time finding your purpose or setting direction for your leadership, ask yourself,

What makes me sing? Your answer reveals what brings you joy.
What makes me cry? Your answer reveals what touches your heart.
What makes me dream? Your answer reveals what sparks your imagination.
What makes me excel? Your answer reveals your strengths.
What makes me different? Your answer reveals your uniqueness.

The more questions you can answer, the greater the number of clues you'll have to help you reveal your purpose as a leader.

It takes time to learn about yourself, but it also takes effort to remain true to yourself. People will ask you to depart from the path that's right for you. But the better you know yourself and the truer you are to yourself, the greater your success will be as a leader. Benjamin Disraeli, one of Britain's great prime ministers, wrote, "I have brought myself, by long meditation, to the conviction that a human being with a settled purpose must accomplish it, and that nothing can resist a will which will stake even existence upon its fulfillment."

As I write this, I am sixty-seven years old, and the fulfillment of my purpose is still unfolding before me. My dreams are getting clearer to me, but I haven't achieved all of them yet. I hope that in the coming years, I will continue to have a sense of anticipation and joy as I seek to fulfill my purpose. The key for me is the same as it is for you: be yourself. No one is better qualified to be you than *you*. God only made one of you, so be yourself and do what he created you for.

4. It Is Said That to Be a Good Leader You Must First Be a Good Follower. Does This Maxim Hold True at All Times? If So, at What Point Does a Follower Become a Leader?

This question reveals a common misconception about leading and following. It assumes that it's either-or. It's not. It's both all the time. Nobody does only one or the other. It's an interplay that leaders must navigate from moment to moment. In many situations I take the lead. I cast vision and set direction for my organizations. But often I become the follower when deferring to the expertise of people in my organization.

Watch the interplay of people during a meeting. In a healthy environment, different people take the lead based on the situation and the skills needed in the moment. Only egotistical leaders believe they must lead in any and every situation.

The best leaders know what it's like to follow and have learned how to do it. And they are willing to learn how to follow well before trying to lead. Aristotle asserted, "Who would learn to lead must... first of all learn to obey." That's why leadership-intensive institutions like the United States Military Academy at West Point teach followership first.

Good followers add value to an organization. They focus well and do their best to make their team and organization better. They strive for excellence in their work. They spot problems and volunteer to fix them. And they champion new ideas.

You might expect followership to be valued in a military setting, but it has value in leadership in every setting. For example, when asked what advice he would give to talented young conductors, octogenarian Lorin Maazel, conductor of the Munich Philharmonic Orchestra, advised, "If they want to learn to become very good, they should learn how to become good followers. Sit in the orchestra and learn how depressing it is to find yourself trying to follow someone you cannot respect either professionally or personally."[25]

Successful followership is a learned skill, just as leadership is. If you want to be a good leader, understand following, and never forget what it's like to sit in the follower's chair.

5. I'm a Bit Introverted, and I Believe That Being More Outgoing Could Help Me to Be a Leader. How Can I Accept My Personality, Yet Blossom in Connecting with Others?

Because so much of leadership is about working with people, it can be more difficult for some introverts to get started leading. But that doesn't mean that introverts can't lead. They have led well in every industry and area of life. Author Susan Cain points out that billionaire Microsoft founder Bill Gates is an introvert. So is investor Warren Buffett, a friend of his. The United States' greatest president, Abraham Lincoln, was an introvert. So was statesman Mahatma Gandhi.

You don't need to be an extrovert to lead others. However, you may at times have to be more outgoing than you would naturally like to be. John Lilly, former CEO of Mozilla, who is an introvert, forced himself to walk the halls and make eye contact with people after he realized that his not greeting others offended them.[26]

You should not try to change your personality to become a better leader. That will only make you come across as phony. You just need to become your best self by focusing on your gifts and maximizing the best qualities of your temperament. For example, let's look at the two classic introverted temperaments: phlegmatic and melancholic. Phlegmatics are known for their steadiness and their ability as peacemakers. If you're phlegmatic, tap into those qualities to give your team security and stability, and then get people to work together. Melancholics are known for their thinking ability, their creativity, and their attention to detail. If you're melancholic, make the most of those qualities by planning and strategizing.

In addition to using your strengths, you do need to make a deliberate and continuous effort to connect with people. To do that...

1. Understand the Value of Connecting with Others

Few things are more important to the leader-follower relationship than connection. I learned in elementary school how much of an impact this makes from one of my all-time favorite teachers: Mrs. Tacy. She made me feel like the most important and most loved child in the world. She went out of her way to let me know how much she cared. Whenever I missed her class, she would write me a note and encourage me. When I returned to class, she made sure I knew that she was aware I had returned and that she was glad to see me. And it wasn't because she singled me out. She made every kid in her class feel that way.

If you want to connect with people, never forget how important it is and work at it every day. People don't care how much you know until they know how much you care. It may sound corny but it is true.

2. Connect with Others Using Your Strengths

As a young leader, I began to work at connecting with people. To do that, I imitated other connectors whom I admired. While it was a good idea to learn from them, it was a mistake to try to be like them. It was a real breakthrough for me when I realized I had strengths that I could use to build rapport and relationships with people. Today I rely on these five qualities every day when working with people, whether one on one, in a meeting, or onstage:

- **Humor:** I enjoy a good laugh and I don't mind being the butt of the joke.
- **Authenticity:** I am myself in all situations, and I don't teach anything I don't live or believe.
- **Confidence:** I feel good about myself and I believe strongly in people.
- **Hope:** I naturally lift up and encourage people, and I love to do it.
- **Simplicity:** I'm pragmatic, not intellectual. I don't try to impress people with big words or complex sentences. I want to connect with people, so I keep it simple.

I don't know what your strengths are, but you have some. What are your top five? Are you using them? Have you found a way to make who you are work for you?

Leading Different Personalities

Which personality type are you? Each one has it own strengths:

The most natural leaders: Choleric
The most loyal leaders: Phlegmatic
The most gifted leaders: Melancholic
The most loved leaders: Sanguine

Make the most of your personality type.

---

3. Ask Good Leaders to Give You Feedback

If you want to learn how to make the most of your strengths and leverage the best traits of your personality type, seek out feedback from other leaders. I did that a lot. Not only did I study good leaders and connectors, I sought their advice about leadership, and whenever possible I asked them to give me specific feedback on my communication. People who are not good at leadership and communication may be able to tell when you aren't connecting, but only good connectors can tell you why.

As Stephen Covey said, "It takes humility to seek feedback. It takes wisdom to understand it, analyze it and appropriately act on it." But it is definitely worth it. Only by being yourself and building on your strengths can you become a better leader.

> "It takes humility to seek feedback. It takes wisdom to understand it, analyze it and appropriately act on it."
> —*Stephen Covey*

6. What Advice Would You Give to an Aspiring Leader Trying to Take the First Steps into Leadership?

My best piece of advice would be to try to take the long view of leadership. Here's why I say this: when I started off in my career, people didn't think much of me. I was very eager, and I had lots of ideas, and I worked hard, but when you're young, people don't think you're very good. And they don't give you much credit. When I was in that situation, I wanted to stand up and say, "Excuse me. I know I'm not real good but I'm better than you think." But you can't do that. You have to prove yourself and earn credibility.

If you work hard, learn how to connect with people, develop credibility, and prove yourself every day, after a while people will begin to believe in you. You will have influence, and you will be able to get things done. And here's what's really ironic. Lead well long enough, and people will shift from giving you *no* credit, to giving you *proper* credit, to giving you *too much* credit. Today people think I'm better than I actually am.

So try not to worry too much about what people think about you. Do your best. Work hard. Keep growing. And eventually you'll be able to make a positive impact as a leader.

7. What's the First Thing a Leader Should Do When Brought in from the Outside to Be Responsible for a Group or Department?

Whenever you take on the responsibility to lead a new team, it's a challenge, whether you are an experienced leader or a novice. But I believe there are five things you can do to get off on the right foot and set up the team for success:

1. Strengthen Relationships

I've already discussed the importance of connecting with people in this chapter. You do that so you can strengthen relationships and start building the team. You do that by putting people first. FedEx founder Fred W. Smith understood this. He said, "Federal Express, from its inception, has put its people first, both because it is right to do so and because it is good business as well. Our corporate philosophy is succinctly stated: People-Service-Profit."

The quickest way to build relationships is to try to get to know and understand each person on your team. To understand the mind of an individual, look at what that person has already achieved. To understand the heart of a person, look at what he or she aspires to do. If you have a handle on people's history and aspirations, you've gone a long way to getting to know them.

2. Earn People's Trust

You cannot lead a team if you do not have the team members' trust. Michael Winston, former managing director and chief leadership officer for Countrywide Financial Corporation, asserts, "Effective leaders ensure that people feel strong and capable. In every major survey on practices of effective leaders, trust in the leader is essential if other people are going to follow that person over time. People must experience the leader as believable, credible, and trustworthy."

3. Position Team Members Properly

It is the leader's responsibility to position team members where they add the most value and have the greatest chance for success. Doing that serves them individually as well as helping the team to perform at its best.

In my book *The 17 Indisputable Laws of Teamwork*, I describe the Law of the Niche, which says all players have a place where they add the most value. How do you figure out where each team member fits? By getting to know his or her strengths and weaknesses. If a leader doesn't know what his players' strengths and weaknesses are, he cannot hand off responsibilities to them. And for that matter, if a leader doesn't know his own strengths and weaknesses, he *will not* hand off responsibilities to his team.

When you take over a team, if you did nothing other than put each player in his or her strength zone, you would greatly increase the productivity and success of the team. It can make a huge difference in a very short time.

4. Create Clear Expectations

Another fairly quick way to positively affect a team is to give the entire team as well as each individual player clear expectations when it comes to performance and goals. Author Denis Waitley asserts, "Motivation is always in direct proportion to the level of expectation." In contrast, not knowing what's expected of us is confusing and demotivating. We all want to have the "win" defined for us.

> "Motivation is always in direct proportion to the level of expectation."
> —*Denis Waitley*

It's always been my experience that if I expect great things from my people, they'll go to great lengths to keep from disappointing me. Good people always rise to your level of expectation.

5. Determine People's Capacity

As every coach knows, most people do not push themselves to their capacity. In fact, if you look at the research that Gallup has done, you find that an overwhelming number of people are downright disengaged at work. It is the leader's job to try to change that. Gallup identifies people's not working in their strengths as the primary reason for disengagement at work, so if you have put people in their strength zones you've already put them on a good path to better performance. If you've communicated what is expected, you've helped them even more. What's left? To motivate and inspire them to achieve, and give them a safe place to fail.

If you encourage people to strive to go farther than they ever have, and you give them the freedom to fail, they will take risks, and you will help them to determine what their true capacity is. That's no small thing. Daniel H. Pink says, "One source of frustration in the workplace is the frequent mismatch between what people must do and what people can do. When what they must do exceeds their capabilities, the result is anxiety. When what they must do falls short of their capabilities, the result is boredom. But when the match is just right, the results can be glorious."

8. How Do You Find Balance Between Leading Others and Producing?

When I started in my career, I wasn't trying to lead anyone. In fact I didn't think about leadership at all. I simply tried to get things done. I focused on reaching people and trying to grow my church. In other words, I was a producer, and if you had asked me, I would have said that leadership was producing.

I look back now and recognize that I was a Level 3 leader, based on the 5 Levels of Leadership. And there's nothing wrong with that. Level 3 is where you develop credibility.

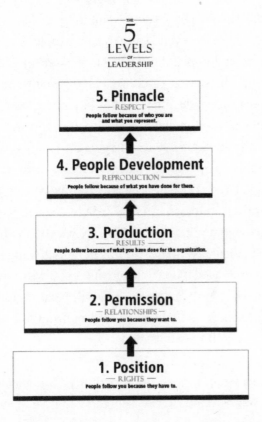

Leadership is often the result of a person's being productive. That's often why people are willing to follow you. If you're good at what you do, motivated people want to know why. They want to watch you and learn from you. They're willing to take your direction, because they hope you can make them better. That's where leadership often starts.

Let's say you're a highly productive person and others begin to recognize that you're good at what you do, and they start asking for your help, even though you have no official leadership responsibilities yet. What do you do? Helping others will take your time. It may reduce your productivity. Will you help them, even though it becomes . more difficult for you to take care of your own responsibilities and get your work done? Many people don't want to be bothered. But let's say ' you love what you do and you desire to help people. So you give them some of your time and pick up the slack by working either longer or smarter. During this season you're probably going to be spending 90 percent of your time producing and only 10 percent leading.

If you work in an organization that recognizes and rewards producers who help the team, you will probably be given some leadership responsibilities. However, you may receive those on top of your responsibilities. (And this will almost certainly be true if you are an entrepreneur or self-employed.) This is where you need to begin learning how to manage producing and leading. Maybe the balance shifts from ninety-ten to eighty-twenty. At this point two things become critical: priorities and delegation. At some point you will run out of hours in your day and days in your week. You will have to stop doing some things and start delegating others. To start figuring out what tasks you can shift, ask yourself these questions:

• **What am I *required* to do personally?** Some tasks cannot be delegated. If you own a business, you know that you have a responsibility to the organization to help it succeed. The buck stops with you. If you work for someone else, there are things your boss requires you to do personally. Ask what *must* be done that *only* you can do and that cannot be delegated. These responsibilities must remain high on your priority list. As I prepared to accept the last leadership position in which I worked for someone else, I asked what tasks only I could do. These I did, and I delegated nearly everything else.

- **What gives the organization the greatest *return*?** Some of the things you do return great value to the organization because they use your greatest strengths. These are the things in your production zone, and you should never delegate them to someone else. For example, I never ask someone else to speak for me. This is my sweet spot. It adds value to people, generates revenue, and increases opportunities for my organizations. I will continue speaking as long as these things are true.

- **What *rewards* me personally?** There are certain tasks that we simply enjoy doing. If they bring a high return, great. If not, we need to let them go. For example, early in my career, I loved spending time looking at metrics and analyzing stats. I could do it all day because it was like a drug to me. But did it give a high return? No. Was it required of me? No. Could someone else do it? Yes. So I had to stop doing it. Truth be told, this is where people get tripped up. They keep doing things they enjoy that they shouldn't be. If you want to be productive, you should try to learn to get joy from what gives the greatest return and discipline yourself to do those things.

> If you want to be productive, you should try to learn to get joy from what gives the greatest return and discipline yourself to do those things.

- **What *reproduces* productivity and leadership in others?** When most people think of delegation, they focus on the benefit to themselves. They understand that it frees up their time to take on additional responsibilities, like leading. And that's good. But there is another benefit of delegating: it allows others to grow in their ability to produce or lead. In the beginning this can actually take up more of your time. But in the long run, it pays off not only for you but also for the organization and the people you develop.

As your leadership ability and responsibilities increase, the balance between the time you spend leading and the time you spend producing will evolve. If you are a great equipper and developer of people—a

Level 4 leader—you may get to where you are spending 90 percent of your time leading and reproducing leaders and only 10 percent of your time actually producing. However, if at any point you begin to lose credibility with your team or the person you work for, you will need to shift more time and attention back to producing. Productivity is the engine that drives your credibility and leadership.

Questions to Ask Before Delegating

As you delegate to others, consider these questions from my friend Bobb Biehl:

1. **Exactly *what* needs to be done?** People cannot hit a hidden target. When you give someone a task, define what needs to be done as precisely as possible. People need to know what a win is.

2. ***Why* does it need to be done?** How do you avoid being constantly drawn back into the process when you delegate something? By telling *why*. When people know why, they are better able to make decisions.

3. ***When* does it need to be done?** Nothing motivates like a deadline. Besides, everyone likes a sense of completion. People won't get it if they don't know when they've finished a task.

4. ***Who* is the best person to do it?** Always try to delegate to people's strengths. You want to set people up for success and help the team to win.

5. ***How well* must it be done?** Not all tasks are created equal. Washing a car doesn't need to be done with the same precision as brain surgery, and to demand the same standards for both is a waste of time and energy. Establish standards according to the importance of the task. In addition, for delegating something I have been doing myself, my general rule of thumb is that if someone can do a job at least 80 percent as well as I would, I shouldn't be doing it myself anymore.

9. I'm Always Worried About Hurting People's Feelings or Worried About What They Will Think of Me. What Can I Do to Overcome This and Become a Strong Leader?

As long as you're overly concerned about what other people think of you, you won't be able to become a strong leader. I say that because I used to be a people pleaser and I cared too much about what others thought of me. When I started in my career, I often knew what to do, but I didn't do it. I had clarity, but not confidence.

The key to my change was deciding to do what was best, not what was best for me. I had to believe in the cause more than in my comfort. I had to live for a purpose bigger than myself. I had to be willing to take the heat so that I could move people forward. Here's how this works:

- Believing in the cause creates your conviction.
- Believing in your vision fuels your inspiration.
- Believing in your people builds your motivation.

Once you possess enough conviction to keep you from worrying about what others think, you will be willing and able to set the standards necessary for you to lead effectively. When I arrived at Skyline in San Diego as its leader, the organization had been on a plateau for many years. How was I able to get it growing again? I raised the standards for leadership: I expected better results from each leader; I insisted that everyone train new leaders; I also let go of some staff members and hired better leaders. Did all these things make me popular with the staff? No. But they helped the organization grow. In the time I was there, it more than tripled in size.

It is the job of the leader to determine the standards for the people he leads. As leader, I can never forget that. I must...

Set the standards,
Teach the standards,
Live the standards,
Lead others to stretch to the standards.

If I don't, both I and the organization will drift into mediocrity—and then go down from there.

To be an effective leader, you must listen to others, and consider their thoughts and ideas, but do what's right for the organization and the people according to your personal values and the highest standards.

10. How Does an Emerging Leader Establish Leadership Confidence Without Affirmation?

Confidence is important for a leader, as I indicated in my answer to the previous question. If you've read *The 21 Irrefutable Laws of Leadership*, you're familiar with the Law of the Big Mo, which says that momentum is a leader's best friend. What turns the key to momentum and gets it started? Often it's the leader's confidence!

Confidence makes it possible for leaders to take risks and speak up. It empowers them to go first when they need to. It helps them tackle big problems and overcome failure. Let's face it: leadership is often messy and difficult. Confidence makes it possible for leaders to keep moving forward in spite of this.

Confidence also sets individuals apart. Confident people stand out from the crowd. Confident leaders provide certainty to uncertain people and security to insecure people. People migrate to confident leaders. People want to follow others who know where they're going. Their confidence gives the people who follow them confidence. Together they are more likely to overcome adversity.

Unfortunately, many young leaders have to function in environments where they receive limited guidance and even less affirmation.

So many leaders must learn to develop confidence on their own. That can be difficult, but it's not impossible. If you desire to improve your leadership confidence, do the following:

1. Spend Time with People Who Give You Confidence

Many times we lack confidence because the people we spend the most time with would rather take us down a notch than lift us up. They're like Charlie Brown's friend Lucy in the *Peanuts* comic strip by Charles M. Schulz. In one strip she tells him, "You, Charlie Brown, are a foul ball in the line drive of life! You're in the shadow of your own goal posts! You are a miscue! You are three putts on the eighteenth green! You are a seven-ten split in the tenth frame! You are the dropped rod and reel in the lake of life! You are a missed free throw, a shanked nine iron and a called third strike! Do you understand? Have I made myself clear?" With friends like that, who needs enemies?

If people in your life make you feel discouraged and tentative, you need to spend less time with them and more time with people who want to see you win and express that to you. I had to do that early in my career. I broadened my circles. And when I found someone who encouraged me, I went out of my way to spend time with him. You should too.

2. Find a Way to Get a Few Wins Under Your Belt

Few things give us confidence like a win. My dad understood this. When I was a kid, I used to wrestle my brother Larry, who is almost two years older than I am. When we were growing up, Larry was bigger and stronger than I, and when we wrestled, Larry always won. Dad could see that this was starting to become discouraging to me, so one day as we pushed back the couch to set up our wrestling area, Dad announced, "I'm going to wrestle John tonight."

I got down on the floor with my dad, and we started to battle each other. Much to my amazement, I was doing well against him. No matter what Dad tried, I was able to work my way out of it and he wasn't able to pin me.

Dad and I wrestled every night. And every night I was able to fight Dad off. Not once was he able to pin me.

Larry watched this go on for a week, and he could barely stand it. He was dying to jump back into the "ring" with me. And Dad finally let him. But guess what? Larry seldom beat me again. The wins Dad put under my belt were enough to give me confidence, and confidence had been all I lacked.

If your confidence isn't what it needs to be, find ways to rack up a few wins. Start with easy ones if you need to. For that matter, you can also make a list of past victories to help you develop (or regain) confidence. Even the best of leaders sometimes feel low and need to remember past victories to give them a boost so they can move forward.

3. Quit Comparing Yourself to Others

One of the things most detrimental to people's confidence is comparing themselves to others. If you are not a naturally confident person or you have a glass-is-half-empty type of personality, you will most likely compare your worst to others' best and find yourself lacking. Don't do it! Others are often not as good as we give them credit for, and we are all too aware of our weaknesses. As a result, the comparison is distorted. Besides, each of us is a unique individual with something to contribute to this world. Instead of comparing yourself to others, focus on being your best you.

4. Specialize Until You're Special

That leads to the final thing I would suggest you do to gain confidence. Become really great at something. If you specialize in doing something based on one of your top strengths, you not only add value to your team, you also find it easier to believe in yourself.

I learned this lesson on the basketball court when I was a kid. Basketball was my first love. I still vividly remember being in fourth grade and watching the high school basketball team being announced at the first game I attended. From that moment I was hooked. After that I spent every spare moment shooting hoops.

What I discovered was that my best skill on the court wasn't handling the basketball, grabbing rebounds, or playing defense. It was shooting. So that became my focus. In particular, I practiced thousands of foul shots. By the time I played in high school, I was the most consistent free throw shooter on the team. And when we were in pressure situations in a game, I was confident in my shooting.

If you want to gain confidence, become an expert in something. Develop a valuable skill. Become an expert on your product. Learn everything there is to know about your customers. It can be nearly anything—if it helps the team to succeed and it gives you confidence, it's a win for everybody.

There is no one clear path to leadership. There is no simple checklist for becoming a leader. Each person's journey is different. In my case, I needed to learn how to lead in order to be successful in my career, but I wasn't aware of that need when I got started. In fact, in the late sixties and early seventies, leadership wasn't a concept that was on many people's radar. Instead people studied management.

It wasn't until I presided over my first board meeting that I got a sense of who was leading the meeting—and it wasn't me. I came in with an agenda and several changes I wanted to make in the organization. Before I could really launch into any of it, a farmer named Claude started to talk, and everyone else started to listen. He took us through the items he thought were important, everyone followed his lead, and before I knew it, the meeting was over. Claude didn't do anything bossy or unpleasant. He simply wanted to get things done and acted as he probably always had during such meetings.

After a couple of meetings like this, I realized that if I wanted the people in the board meeting to address the issues that were important to me, I needed those issues to come from the leader—Claude. So about a week before the next meeting, I went to visit Claude out on the farm. We chatted, I helped with chores, and I just happened to mention a couple of the issues that were important to me. When Claude heard them, he said, "We should probably bring those up at our next board meeting." I told Claude I thought that was a good idea. For the next three years, if there was something I thought was important, I brought it up with Claude, and he made it happen. Why? Because he was the person with influence at the church, and I was just a kid with a job title.

I learned many great lessons in my first leadership position, the most important of which was that leadership has to be earned. Leaders have to grow into their roles, and if the role becomes more demanding, the leader has to keep growing. Leadership is never a right. It's a privilege and a responsibility. But it's one that is open to anyone who's willing to work hard enough to get it.

> I learned many great lessons in my first leadership position, the most important of which was that leadership has to be earned.

Questions Related to Resolving Conflict and Leading Challenging People

1. How can a leader...
    - Move an individual from unteachable to teachable?
    - Demand the change of a bad attitude from an employee?
    - Lead someone with a passive-aggressive personality who is loyal and effective, but is hindering the team?
    - Handle an angry employee?
    - Deal with a person who does not want to be led?

2. How do you raise the bar when people have gotten used to settling for mediocrity?

3. How do you motivate an unmotivated person?

4. How do you deal with people who start things but never finish?

5. How can leaders help individuals move past their mistakes, filter out negative self-talk, and get on a path of success toward a better future?

6. At what point do you turn your energy away from dissenters and low performers and focus on those who want to grow?

7. How do you inspire your team to make its current work a career and something to be proud to do, and not just another job with a paycheck?

8. How does one lead people who are more knowledgeable, or superior leaders, when put in charge of them?

9. How long do you push someone's potential when they are not reaching it?

10. How do you know a relationship is broken and how can you save it?

7

How Do I Resolve Conflict and Lead Challenging People?

I mentioned in chapter four that the most-asked questions I receive relate to self-leadership. The area in which I receive the second-greatest number of questions is that of dealing with conflict and leading challenging people. This is one of the most difficult areas for most leaders. You can do all the right things, but there is no guarantee others will change, succeed, or do well.

Let me be very frank: the answers in this chapter will work only with people who possess some desire to work with you. People who do not want to follow or be productive members of the team will not change. And that doesn't make you a bad leader. It just means you have someone who's bad for the team and organization. You only cross into bad leadership if you make the choice to keep someone on the team when you shouldn't.

Too often, leaders wait. They don't like to make these difficult decisions. They hope people will change on their own instead of challenging them and offering them a pathway to change. When people on the team are creating conflict or dragging the team down, many leaders think, *I've failed them somehow. Let me try harder. Let me try something different. Let me move them into a different position. Maybe things will turn around.*

This rarely works. I learned this lesson from my older brother Larry, but in a different context: finances. He taught me that your first loss should be your last loss. Most business leaders take a loss, then throw good money after bad in the hopes of making it up. It rarely works. Larry taught me that it's wiser to cut your losses. Don't compound them by waiting.

The same can be said of decisions related to people. Everyone deserves our best shot as leaders to help them succeed. But they don't deserve repeated chances—especially at the expense of others on the team. Nobody likes making these hard decisions, but they must be made, and the sooner the better. Good leaders are direct and decisive in these matters. Ask yourself: is this best for the team? If keeping someone who's difficult isn't, get him or her off the team.

1. How Can a Leader
...Move an Individual from Unteachable to Teachable?
...Demand the Change of a Bad Attitude from an Employee?
...Lead Someone with a Passive-Aggressive Personality Who Is Loyal and Effective, But Is Hindering the Team?
...Handle an Angry Employee?
...Deal with a Person Who Does Not Want to Be Led?

Any time you have difficulty with people you lead, whether it's because of a negative attitude, poor performance, lack of cooperation, or some other issue, you need to start a process then, and that process is the same for nearly every situation. Before I lay that out for you, I want to point out two questions you need to ask before you get started:

Can they change? This deals with ability.
Will they change? This deals with attitude.

Most of the questions people asked about dealing with others in this chapter do not relate to ability. They relate to attitude.

For this process to be successful, when you ask people to change, the answer to both questions has to be yes. It can't be either/or. I've known people with great ability but a bad attitude, and I've known people with a great attitude and poor ability. If people are able and willing to change, there's a chance you can be successful.

1. Meet Privately ASAP to Discuss Their Behavior

As I've already said, most people wait too long to address an issue with an employee. That's a mistake. Missionary doctor Albert Schweitzer asserted, "Truth has no special time of its own. Its hour is now—always." If you have a problem with someone, do something about it as quickly as you can.

Meet with the person privately and level with them with integrity and honesty. Sit down and very clearly lay out what the issue is, giving specific, tangible examples of the undesirable actions or behaviors. Don't be vague. Don't use secondhand reports. Don't attribute bad motives to them, because they will only get defensive. In fact, go into the conversation assuming their motives are good. This is more likely to make them open to change and willing to make corrections. And be sure to explain how their actions are negatively affecting the organization, the team, or you.

One more thing. Never go into one of these meetings angry. If you do, you greatly reduce your chances of success. Psychologist William James said, "Whenever you're in conflict with someone, there is one factor that can make the difference between damaging your relationship and deepening it. The factor is attitude." If your attitude is positive, your mind-set is to give them the benefit of the doubt, and you truly want to help the person, you give yourself the best odds for a positive resolution.

> "Whenever you're in conflict with someone, there is one factor that can make the difference between damaging your relationship and deepening it. The factor is attitude."
> —William James

2. Ask for Their Side of the Story

Peter Drucker observed, "Erroneous assumptions can be disastrous." I'm a pretty good judge of people, but I still sometimes read situations wrong. I misunderstand something that happened, make wrong assumptions, or don't realize I'm missing an important piece of information. Sometimes circumstances such as a personal tragedy are temporarily prompting unwanted behavior, and the person simply needs help or understanding. That's why you don't want to go in with guns blazing. You might be wrong.

3. Try to Come to a Place of Agreement

At this point it's time to find out if they agree with you. Former secretary of state Dean Acheson stated, "Negotiation in the classic diplomatic sense assumes parties more anxious to agree than to disagree." That's the right attitude to bring into the process.

When I've met with people in this situation, I've had some look at me and say, "You're right. This is a problem that I have." It can be very humbling for them, but it opens them up to change, and that's ideal. Often you can help someone with that attitude.

However, I've also had many people say, "No, it's someone else's problem." When that happens I tell them, "I believe I'm right and this is your problem. I'm going to give you a week to think about it. We'll meet again and discuss it." My hope is that they'll give it some honest thought and maybe ask people who know them well and will be honest with them.

After a week has gone by, we meet and I ask, "Do you agree that this is your problem?" If they have a change of heart and agree with me, we can move forward to the next step because they've taken responsibility. If they still don't agree, I say, "You may not agree with what I've just said. But you will have to agree to change and follow my guidelines if you want to remain on the team. And I'm going to hold you accountable."

4. Set Out a Future Course of Action with a Deadline

No matter whether people agree with you or not, you must lay out a specific course of action for them to take. Once again, be very specific. Indicate any actions they must not take or behaviors they must not exhibit, starting immediately. If there are action steps they will need to follow through on, lay those out and put deadlines on them. And make sure they understand. Put your requirements into writing if needed. If you don't both agree on what needs to happen in the future, you will both be frustrated.

5. Validate the Value of the Person and Express Your Commitment to Help

Before you finish your meeting, let them know that you care about them and genuinely desire a positive resolution to the situation. Tell them how you will help them. Goethe recommended, "Treat people as if they were what they ought to be, and you help them become what they are capable of becoming."

*   *   *

Sometimes the greatest value a leader can add to other people comes through telling them the truth, showing them where they can grow, and then helping them change. Some people spend years on a job being resented by their boss and fellow employees, but are never told about their problem or given a chance to change and grow. As a leader, you have the chance to help them.

> Sometimes the greatest value a leader can add to other people comes through telling them the truth, showing them where they can grow, and then helping them change.

Sitting down with people and telling them where they fall short isn't easy. And there's no guarantee that they will acknowledge their problem or change. There's a strong chance that you will have to let them go. If you are having a hard time making that decision, ask yourself this question: "If I needed to hire new people, knowing what I know now, would I hire these individuals?"

If the answer is yes—keep them.

If the answer is no—let them go.

If the answer is maybe—reevaluate in three months.

If the answer is that you don't know, give yourself three months. If the answer is still that you don't know, the answer is really no. Your emotions are making it difficult for you to accept a hard decision.

Fred Smith, one of my mentors, said, "Whenever I am tempted not to act in a difficult personnel situation, I ask myself, 'Am I holding back for my own personal comfort or for the good of the organization?' If I am doing what makes me comfortable, I am embezzling. If doing what is good for the organization also happens to make me comfortable, that's wonderful. But if I am treating irresponsibility irresponsibly, I must remember that two wrongs do not make a right."

As a leader, you owe it to the rest of the team to make these tough choices. That's what you get paid for.

2. How Do You Raise the Bar When People Have Gotten Used to Settling for Mediocrity?

The first question in this chapter dealt primarily with attitude issues. This is more of a performance issue. I think any time the team isn't performing, the leader has to look at himself first. I need to examine whether I am part of the problem. Am I setting a bad example by settling for mediocrity personally? Is that part of the problem? Or have I lowered my expectations so far that people just assume that average is OK? If either of these things is true, I need to go back to the question in chapter four: what must I do to lead myself successfully? I can't raise the bar for others if I haven't raised the bar for myself.

> I can't raise the bar for others if I haven't raised the bar for myself.

If you as a leader are pushing to reach your maximum potential, you can begin to look at the people you lead and start asking them questions:

• **Are you reaching your maximum potential?** This is often an awareness issue. Many people don't understand that they can do much more than they are currently doing. They may not even have reaching their potential as a goal. Help them see the possibilities.

• **Would you like to do better?** You can find out a lot about a person by hearing their answer to this question. If they answer yes, you may be able to help them. If they answer no, they can't even help themselves.

• **Do you know how to reach your maximum potential?** Many people don't have a clue about how to be more successful. They have the desire, but not the knowledge. This is a case where a "no" answer is actually a good thing. If they don't know the path forward, you may be able to show it to them.

- **Can I help you?** One of the most rewarding roles leaders have is that of coach and mentor. When people are teachable and open to growth, helping them succeed can be highly rewarding.

One of the things you as a leader need to help your people understand is that nothing good comes out of being average professionally. You can't build a business or make a difference by being average. It's OK to be average in many areas of your life. You can be an average golfer and still have golf as an enjoyable hobby. You can be an average cook and still keep your family fed. You can be an average driver and get from point A to point B. But you can't settle for mediocre in your marriage, for example, and expect it to remain solid. And you can't be mediocre in your profession and expect to be rewarded for it.

In a practical sense, one of the best ways to raise the bar for people is to do it incrementally. For example, if you are a real estate broker with a lot of agents in your office and most of them make only three sales a year, challenge them to do four. That's a very reasonable increase that most people will believe they can do. If you set the goal, give them an incentive to reach it, help them create a plan to achieve it, and check in with them along the way, most of them will be able to achieve it.

The beauty of incremental challenges is that they increase the confidence of the people who achieve them. And they inspire everyone else who has been average. They give them hope. That's why every time someone gets a win, you should tell their story. It rewards that person and motivates those in the middle to perform better. The top producers don't need motivation. They are already motivated and performing well. Everyone else needs it.

An incremental challenge also helps the organization when it has a lot of people. If every person grows a little, the organization grows a lot. If you can get a lot of people improving, it can have a tremendous impact overall.

3. How Do You Motivate an Unmotivated Person?

When I started out in leadership, I thought I could change people. Now I realize I can't. People must change themselves. That doesn't mean that I have no responsibility to people in my organization in the area of motivation. There are still things I can do. I can work to create an environment and culture where motivation is valued and rewarded. Here are the ways I do that:

Start with Motivated People

The best way to create a culture of motivation is to start with as many motivated people as you can. The Law of Magnetism in *The 21 Irrefutable Laws of Leadership* states, "Who you are is who you attract." If you want people on your team to be motivated, you must be motivated yourself. People do what people see. I have to live it before I expect it from anyone else.

You should also hire motivated people. That sounds obvious, but you might be surprised how many leaders leave this trait out of the equation when looking for team members. Many focus too much on just talent or skill. Even the leaders who recognize the importance of attitude sometimes miss motivation. And then they wonder why their people aren't performing at a higher level.

Understand the Connection between Relationships and Motivation

People are motivated by leaders who connect with them and treat them like human beings. If you are a people person, this may sound painfully obvious to you, yet some leaders still miss it. I once knew a leader who referred to all the people on his team as "ding-a-lings."

Hire Motivated People

How can you identify motivated people? They usually have several of the following traits:

1. They exhibit a positive attitude.
2. They can articulate specific goals for their life.
3. They are initiators.
4. They have a proven track record of success.

Look for these traits when looking for new team members.

He was constantly saying things like "I told the ding-a-lings what to do, but of course they didn't do it," and "I've got to go meet with the ding-a-lings." It was clear that he believed everyone was below him. His contempt for people was apparent to everyone who worked for him. Few things are more demotivating than working for someone who disrespects you.

Give Each Person a Reputation to Uphold

People often go farther than they think they can go when someone else thinks they can. One way to show people that you believe in them and in the possibility of success for their future is to give them a reputation to uphold.

Ask yourself what's special, unique, and wonderful about each person on your team. All people have talents, skills, and positive traits that make them valuable to the team. Figure out what they are and then share them with others. The more you validate people for the good things they do—or could do—the more they want to do them. Not only does this motivate them to perform in their strength, it also encourages an environment where people say positive things about one another.

Reward What You Want Done

I'm well known for my books on the laws of leadership, teamwork, and growth. Recently I came across Grandma's Law. It says, "If you eat your vegetables, you can have dessert." It's amazing how well this works with kids. Why? Because most people will work for a reward they desire. If you want to create an environment where people are motivated, give them reasons to get things done.

I love the story of the salesman who sat looking through the window of a hotel restaurant. Outside raged a blinding snowstorm.

"Do you think the roads will be clear enough in the morning to travel?" he asked his waiter.

"That depends," the waiter replied. "Are you on salary or commission?"

Rewards are motivating. Rules, consequences, and punishment don't do anything to get people going. They merely keep people from doing their worst. If you want people's best, give them incentives for performance.

4. How Do You Deal with People Who Start Things but Never Finish?

The bookends of success are starting and finishing. Some people never start. If people don't have the discipline to do what they must when they need to do it, they have no shot at success. Good things in life don't float to you. However, some people are in love with starting things, but never finish them. I know someone who loves to start but never finishes. He's had seventeen different

> The bookends of success are starting and finishing.

jobs. He says, "I've finally found something I want to do." That new job usually lasts about three or four months. He's a perpetual optimist, but only about things he hasn't done yet.

As a leader you can help people to finish better by helping them understand what happens when they don't follow through and finish something:

They Lose the Reward of Finishing

Anyone who has accomplished things in life understands that 90 percent of the rewards in life come on the back end, not the front end. A great sense of personal satisfaction comes from completing a job and doing it well. There is a great sense of camaraderie and joy among team members when they work together to accomplish a goal. And of course the monetary rewards also come from finishing. People who never finish anything never experience these rewards, so they don't understand them, and they don't realize that almost all of life's rewards are on the back end.

They Lower Their Self-Esteem

Every time people quit and don't finish something they start, they lose a bit of their self-esteem. Whether they are aware of it or not, they begin to internally label themselves as quitters. I've never found a person with a high self-image who quits all the time. There is a pride in accomplishment that people who quit do not possess. They may show false bravado, but not a deep sense of satisfaction with who they are and what they can do.

They Sabotage Their Own Success

People who never finish often don't understand they are developing a habit that will sabotage their success. Quitting becomes a habit.

And they make excuses. But it's easier to move from failure to success than from excuses to success!

> **It's easier to move from failure to success than from excuses to success.**

My dad drilled into us kids that if we started something, we would have to finish it. He used to say, "When you made the choice to start, you made the choice to finish. It's not two choices; it's one." That kind of mind-set has served my brother Larry, my sister Trish, and me well.

They Lose the Trust and Respect of Others

Quit enough times, and others will think you are unreliable, and that erodes trust. Nobody wants to work with people they cannot trust. Nobody wants to be handcuffed to a quitter. People who blow themselves up will eventually take you with them.

Practical Tips to Help People Become Finishers

To help people learn to finish what they start, do the following:

1. **Show them the big picture:** Help them to see the more positive future they can have if they learn to become finishers.
2. **Give them accountability:** People who have developed the habit of quitting are often unaccountable for their actions. You can change that.
3. **Help them schedule their time:** People who don't finish are often unorganized or undisciplined. They often need tools to help them with scheduling tasks.
4. **Provide a work partner:** Sometimes pairing non-finishers with highly motivated people can help them to follow through. Just be sure you don't bring down a good performer in the process.
5. **Reward only finished work:** It's good to praise effort, but you should never reward it. Give the reward only when the work is done.

People who don't finish what they start often don't recognize the negative impact it has on themselves and others. As a leader, you can help them to understand. Teach them that by starting *and* finishing they are demonstrating that they can handle bigger and better responsibilities. They become candidates for more time, attention, and opportunity from you and the organization because they are demonstrating that they are ready for these things.

5. How Can Leaders Help Individuals Move Past Their Mistakes, Filter Out Negative Self-Talk, and Get on a Path of Success Toward a Better Future?

The ability to deal with difficulties, mistakes, failure, and loss is crucial to people's success. My desire to help people with this has been so strong that I've written two books to teach people how to do it: *Failing Forward* and *Sometimes You Win—Sometimes You Learn.*

Many people get emotionally stuck when they make a mistake or suffer a loss. They often become overwhelmed by regret. That's a problem because, as writer Katherine Mansfield observed, "Regret is an appalling waste of energy.... You can't build on it; it's only good for wallowing in." If the regret takes hold for too long, it can turn into guilt, resentment, and self-pity.

When we experience losses, we need to learn from them and let them go. If we focus on the loss instead, it can bring us down. Here's the difference between people who focus on the loss and those who focus on the lesson:

PEOPLE WHO FOCUS ON THE LOSS	PEOPLE WHO FOCUS ON THE LESSON
Think About What They Did Wrong	Think About What They Can Do Right
Relive the Pain	Put Energy into Healing
Increase Self-Pity	Increase Self-Reliance
Get Emotionally Down	Get Excited
Feel Hopeless	Gain Hope
Get Stuck in the Past	Move Forward Toward the Future

Some losses require time because they cut deeply. We need to grieve. We need time to heal. But many small losses and problems don't warrant much energy. Most of the time we need to learn the lesson from the loss, and then move on.

Teach People the Twenty-Four-Hour Rule

One of the healthiest ways to treat loss is the same way we should treat victory: observe the twenty-four-hour rule. When we experience victory, we should celebrate for no longer than twenty-four hours. When we experience defeat, we should let it get us down for no longer than twenty-four hours. Once you've processed the emotions, it's time to learn from the experience and move on. The quicker you turn your focus from the loss to the lesson, the sooner you will heal. If you remain focused on the loss, it keeps getting worse.

---

6. At What Point Do You Turn Your Energy Away from Dissenters and Low Performers and Focus on Those Who Want to Grow?

As leaders, we often want to take everyone with us. I know I did as a young leader. I was going places, I was excited about it, and I wanted everyone to take the journey with me. But that never happens. Some people can't go with you. Others don't want to. Your job as a leader is to give people a chance to get on board, giving them your best at help-ing them succeed, or to move on without them.

The people you spend most of your time and energy on are the ones who stay. The ones you neglect are the ones who leave. Which would you rather have with you? The high performers who are on board with the vision, or the low performers who criticize you and the organiza-tion? If you give your effort to the negative people, at some point you need to ask yourself:

How much of my energy will I let them take?
How much of my time will I let them take?
How much of my focus will I let them take?
How much of my joy will I let them take?
How much of the resources will I let them take?

Asking these questions makes you realize there is a cost to keeping negative or unproductive people. There are lifters and leaners. Whom do you want on your team?

As I get older, I'm finding that I want to spend my time with people I enjoy. I don't put up with as much as I once did. I have little desire to waste time trying to fulfill other people's agendas. I want to invest in people who grow and who want to make a difference in the lives of others.

If you don't winnow out the dissenters and low performers, you lose people's respect for your leadership. If people are not doing their jobs, they deserve your best shot to help them succeed. When you have given them your best shot, if they're still not doing their best, it's time to make changes.

When I went to San Diego to lead Skyline, I inherited a very weak staff. I did my best to get to know them, to learn their strengths and weaknesses. And I gave my best to help them be successful, but it became clear very quickly that many were not going to be good enough to take Skyline to the next level.

So I developed a strategy. That first year, I let go of a third of the staff and replaced them with people who were high performers and believed in the vision. The next year I let go of the bottom third again and replaced them with better performers. The third year—you guessed it—I let go of the bottom third. Aside from a few exceptions, I had replaced the entire staff in three years.

As a leader, you have to set the standard, and then follow through on it. You have to be willing to make the difficult choices and live with the fallout. My friend Jimmy Blanchard at Synovus did that. Synovus has been voted one of the ten top companies to work for in America. Jimmy Blanchard, who was the CEO, helped to create that. Do you know how he did it? He got rid of the people he believed were hurting the company.

He felt that one of the main problems in the company was that employees were not always being treated well, and he believed the issue was many of the supervisors. So in a meeting with the entire company, he told people that the company wasn't reaching its potential because people were not being valued as they should be. Then he pulled out his cell phone and told everyone in the auditorium that if a supervisor devalued them, they could call him personally to tell him about it, and then he gave out his personal phone number.

Jimmy told me that for the next six months, he received not dozens but hundreds of calls. What he discovered was that the problem kept happening with the same supervisors. So he and the other leaders went to those supervisors and told them that they had to either change or go. It took them about a year and a half to clear out about a third of the supervisors, but it turned the company around. Jimmy said he changed the supervisors slowly, but he changed his people's attitude immediately.

The more experience I've had, the more I've realized that as a leader, you just have to go do what needs to be done. When I have to let someone go, I try to do it in the right way. I appreciate them. I do the right thing financially. And I don't look back. Recently, when I let someone go, he wanted another chance or the opportunity to come back in a lesser role. I said no. If it doesn't work, it doesn't work. Often we know it won't work, but we want to keep the relationship and we give in. That's not good for anybody in the long run. In my early years, I kept people too long. I didn't make courageous decisions. I put my own feelings above what was best for the organization. But I've learned not to do that. Today I'm not the same person I used to be. I'm stronger, more decisive, more courageous. I've quit trying to get everybody to love me. Now I just try to do the right thing.

7. How Do You Inspire Your Team to Make Its Current Work a Career and Something to Be Proud to Do, and Not Just Another Job with a Paycheck?

If people see the work they're currently doing as nothing more than a job for a paycheck, they will become frustrated over time. Almost equally frustrating is targeting a particular position or title and then thinking you've arrived once you receive it. No *job* has a future. Only *people* have a future. If people keep growing, learning, and expanding their potential, their future is bright. If not, it's uncertain at best.

> No *job* has a future. Only *people* have a future.

That's why I often remind people that the greatest threat to tomorrow's success is today's success.

To be successful, I've kept reinventing myself. I've continued to grow, learn, and add to who I am. I started out as a minister. When I realized that to be successful I needed to influence people, I added leadership skills and became a leader. When I began to realize that my communication ability wasn't strong enough, I started to study good speakers and add to my skills until I became an effective communicator. When I realized that you can only take people so far in their growth using speeches and conferences, I learned to write and create resources so I could become an equipper. Then I learned the power of mentoring and became a developer of leaders. Today I've come to appreciate the power of partnership, and I've begun partnering with other leaders and organizations to try to make a difference.

What's next? I have no idea. When I see a growth opportunity to become something more than I currently am, I will seize it and pay the price for the next stage of the journey. That's what all of us need to do.

If you're leading people who have settled into a role or position, whether it's because they are in a comfort zone or because they see their work as just a job, try to help them open their eyes and think beyond today. Help them to realize that a job is never big enough for a human being. We have too much inside us for that. Offer them something beyond their job by doing the following:

Share Your Passion

If you have passion for what you do, you need to share it with your people. A leader's passion is contagious. It can attract other passionate people, and it can spark a flame in people who might not otherwise be passionate. If they can understand and connect with the vision you have and the passion you feel, there's a good chance that they will catch it and become passionate too.

Paint a Picture of a Better Future

As I already mentioned, a job is never big enough for people. They want to do something bigger, something that is worth working for.

People want to make a difference. One of your jobs as a leader is to paint a picture of their future that inspires them to work harder today. Tell them who they can become. Show them what they could some-day be doing. This must be done with integrity, because as leaders, we never want to manipulate people. We just want to help them envision the future.

Show How Their Role Makes a Difference

Too often people don't understand how the tasks they do contribute to the bigger picture. Good leaders help team members understand their role. They help them see how their contribution is making a difference. This gives team members a sense of ownership over the mission, and inspires them to do better work.

Challenge Them to Keep Growing

H. Nelson Jackson said, "I do not believe you can do today's job with yesterday's methods and be in business tomorrow." That's why we need to help people see the value of growing. It is essential not only for the organization's viability, but also for the individual's future. People who make growth their goal—instead of a title, position, sal-ary, or other external target—always have a future.

All of these things have the potential to help a leader inspire someone to invest himself more fully in his work and stop coasting. But every-thing I've just discussed rests on one assumption: that you are passion-ate about your own work. That is essential. People do not follow an uncertain trumpet. They can't catch fire from a leader who has grown cold himself. If you aren't fired up, you are a big part of the problem, and the first person you must address is yourself.

8. How Does One Lead People Who Are More Knowledgeable, or Superior Leaders, When Put in Charge of Them?

If you've been put in charge of a group of people who are stronger than you in leadership or technical ability, here's the good news: you have a position. Here's the bad news: the position won't mean anything to them. They won't follow you because of it.

I learned this in my first leadership position. I was twenty-two. The real leaders in the church were in their forties and had been there for decades. They wouldn't follow me. But that doesn't mean I gave up. Instead I developed a strategy of asking for people's help. If someone pointed out a deficiency in my leadership, I didn't try to convince him that I was right. I agreed with him and asked for his help. Because I was young and didn't try to pretend that I was a better leader, people were willing to help me. Meanwhile I learned as much as I could, worked as hard as I could, and tried to help others as much as I could. As a result, within six months I had started to develop credibility.

If you're not a young leader entering this kind of situation, you may need to take a slightly different tack. First of all, if the team is talented, you can't fool them. You can't fake it. Good leaders will sniff this out instantly. You can't make a mess and then expect the team to bail you out. You'll lose them. You also can't use your position or pull rank and keep their respect. If you try to, they will disdain you and then sabotage you. You need to admit where they're better than you, and look for common ground. If they know that *you* know you're not as good as they are, they may not feel as compelled to keep pointing it out to you.

Your best strategy may be to enlist help from the most influential person on the team. Go to him or her and say, "Look, I know you're more experienced than I am. You have more knowledge. My goal is to help the team win. Can I get your help? When I have a problem, can I come to you for advice? When I need to make a decision for the team, can I talk it over with you? I know that with your help, we can all be successful." If the person says yes, follow through. Ask for advice. Ask for help. And when things go right, publicly give that person credit.

Who Is Most Influential?

It can be very difficult to evaluate leaders who are more gifted and skilled than you are. It's always easier to judge those less talented. So how do you figure out who the main influencer is? Ask these questions:

1. When points are being made, whom does everyone agree with?
2. When questions are asked, whom does everyone look to for answers?
3. When conflict arises, whom does everyone defer to?
4. Who is the person everybody listens to when he or she speaks?

You may not be able to make this determination quickly. You may need to see people interacting in a variety of situations over time. But if you pay attention, you should be able to figure it out.

---

9. How Long Do You Push Someone's Potential When They Are Not Reaching It?

There are hosts of people in this world to whom it's never occurred to try to grow, to strive to reach their potential. They are in survival mode, simply drifting through life. I have no desire to have such people on my team. I want people who want to make a difference and whose desire is to keep improving themselves so they get the opportunity to make a greater impact. Yet for nearly everyone, that is an uphill battle. One of my mentors, consultant Fred Smith, passed this on to me:

Something in human nature tempts us to stay where we're comfortable. We try to find a plateau, a resting place, where we have comfortable stress and adequate finances. Where we have comfortable associations with people, without the intimidation of meeting new people and entering strange situations. Of course, all of us need to plateau for a time. We climb and then plateau for assimilation. But once we've assimilated what we've learned, we climb again. It's unfortunate when we've done our last climb. When we have made our last climb, we are old, whether forty or eighty.

> "When we have made our last climb, we are old, whether forty or eighty."
> —*Fred Smith*

To keep growing toward our potential, we have to be intentional. We have to fight for it. That can be difficult. Not everyone is willing to keep doing it. When people stop growing, I find that it is often for one or more of the following reasons:

Choices

Many people make choices that limit them. They quit a job with great potential because it is difficult. They put themselves into debt and then can't pursue an entrepreneurial opportunity. They choose a fun vacation over a conference that might lead to a personal breakthrough. In life, for everything you gain, you give up something. We can make choices that increase our potential or choices that take away from it.

Time

Most people have a short-term approach to success. They want it now. And even if they are willing to engage in a process, they usually have no idea it will take a long time. So they bail out. They need to

> **"Have patience. All things are difficult before they become easy."**
> —*Saadi*

heed the advice of Persian poet Saadi, who wrote, "Have patience. All things are difficult before they become easy."

I have to admit, I am an impatient person. And I usually have unrealistic expectations about how long something will take. How do I fight against this weakness? I develop systems to help me, and I rely on daily disciplines. By focusing on what I know I should do today, I am able to keep plugging away and continue growing.

Price

Many people think they can rely on talent alone to get them through life. But talent will not carry you to your potential. It's only one part of the equation. Everyone who strives to reach his potential must pay a price—in time, effort, resources, and opportunities missed. Many people fail to pay the price that their potential demands.

Problems

Everybody faces problems, obstacles, and barriers. Some people let those things defeat them. They fail to think creatively when problems arise. They don't have the tenacity to fight through them. Or they lack belief in themselves.

Sometimes all people need is some encouragement. I saw an illustration of this at the 2013 Leadercast event. Former Navy SEAL commander Rorke Denver asked everyone to reach up as high as they could. Once everyone had, he said, "Now reach one inch higher." As I watched, I saw all the arms in the room go up just a bit more. We are literally capable of doing more and going higher than we believe we can.

*   *   *

As a leader, I believe I have a responsibility to help people grow and reach their potential. However, I am not responsible for the outcome. I can do my best to set people up for success, but it's up to them whether or not they do the work to be the best they can be.

That means I need to spend time getting to know what a person can do. I must evaluate their present skills, potential capacities, level of commitment, ability to be motivated, discipline, and intensity. If I am to lead, I owe it to my people to take the time to evaluate well. Only then can I discover the best way to motivate, develop, and equip my people.

Having said that, I also know that most people do not push themselves to their full capacity to reach their potential. My friend Gerald Brooks describes it this way: if life is like an elevator ride, most people will get off one floor lower than they have to. That can be very frustrating, because if you are a caring leader who is concerned about people, you want to see people go as far as they can. Your goal is to help people to reach the highest floor they can. But in the process, it's important that *you* don't get off at a lower floor yourself just because of your desire to help them. You still need to be true to yourself and keep striving to be your best.

If you lead people who are falling short of their potential, you need to start asking why. Have you put them in their strength zone? Are you providing the training and resources they need to be successful? Is there something they need that you're not giving? You always need to make sure you are not the problem before you look to see where the problem is.

After that, you must remember it is their choice, not yours. You can't push people to reach their potential. You can choose to leave the door open for them, but they must walk through. If they choose not to, you're better off spending your time on someone who's hungry and actively wants to grow.

10. How Do You Know a Relationship Is Broken and How Can You Save It?

Good leaders are constantly cultivating and managing relationships with people at work—their peers, their bosses, their employees—plus all their personal relationships outside of their jobs. Any time a relationship is strained, damaged, or broken, they need to address the problem as quickly as possible. When something is broken or a person is hurt, when there's silence between you, the other person almost always assumes the worst. And they start filling any gaps of information with negative assumptions.

How can you tell when a relationship has become broken? These are the most common signs:

• **It's hard to have an honest conversation:** When relationships are in trouble, it becomes difficult to have a normal, honest conversation. If you try to start one, the other person will refuse to engage, or become defensive or combative. They don't want to hear from you. They don't want to talk it out. Maybe they've been so hurt that they just can't handle it.

• **There's a lack of trust:** When relationships begin to break down, suspicion creeps in. The other person begins to question motives. Maybe they feel a sense of injustice or lack of fairness. Whatever trust was originally there begins to deteriorate.

• **There's a lack of passion to continue the relationship:** Eventually the other person stops putting in any effort to build back the relationship or make it work. At this point they often withdraw completely, and it becomes very difficult for you to connect with them. Or if you can manage to get with them, they're mentally or emotionally withdrawn from you. Even if you're together, you're not relating to one another.

*   *   *

When you see these signs, you should try to repair the relationship. That doesn't mean trying to get it back at all costs. Some people sell themselves to try to buy back a broken relationship, and they give away too much. Your goal should be to repair the relationship, but to do it with integrity. Here's what I think it takes to do that:

1. Initiate Fixing the Relationship with Them

When I have a great relationship and it starts to get strained or broken, I feel it's my responsibility to go to the person to see what can be done to fix it. I think it's always the leader's responsibility to be the first to try to mend the relationship. We need to pick up the phone and say, "Hey, can we go to lunch? We need to talk." That doesn't mean it always pays off. But it's hard to rescue a relationship if you don't take responsibility for initiating.

> It's always the leader's responsibility to be the first to try to mend the relationship.

2. Give Them the Benefit of the Doubt

I always go into that conversation assuming that I've done something wrong. I've discovered that if there's hope for helping a relationship come back, the conversation goes better if I'm open and willing to take the blame. So I assume I'm wrong. I'll ask, "Have I offended you? Is there something I've done that's put a strain on our relationship? Is there anything I can do to make amends? Please talk to me."

Sometimes people say, "No, it's not you," and they'll explain what's going on in their life that is causing them to withdraw. Sometimes they say, "Yes, there is. Here's what you did." And they'll talk to me. When that happens, there's a chance to repair the relationship. When that's the case, I ask forgiveness. And even if what I did wasn't wrong, I still apologize for what hurt them. It's difficult to move forward with relational baggage weighing you down.

3. Be Willing to Walk the Second Mile

I believe it is the responsibility of the leader to initiate and to go the second mile in trying to repair a broken relationship. Leaders need to be quick to say, "I'm sorry." They need to be willing to make needed changes. That's a part of leadership.

In relationships, I believe the stronger person is the first one to come back and offer to reconcile. The stronger person is the first to ask for forgiveness. Usually that's the leader. Even if the leader has been the injured party, he needs to initiate. However, the truth is that the weaker person controls the relationship. They always do and they always will.

As a leader you can walk the second mile, but you can't determine the outcome of the attempted reconciliation. There will be times when no matter how much effort you put in, the relationship is never the same as it was before. And you can't be held hostage by that. You have to accept it, because as a leader, you have the responsibility to be a good steward of your team or organization. You cannot allow your personal feelings of not wanting to hurt somebody keep you from doing what's best for the organization. That was hard for me to learn, because I'm so relationally driven.

4. Speak Well of Them Afterward

After I've talked to people and tried to resolve whatever issues we've had, my goal is to have no unfinished business with them. Whether we resolved the issues and mended the relationship, or had to part ways, I don't want there to be any kind of grudge between us, and I want to say only positive things about them. If we see each other on the street, I don't want to avoid them and I don't want them to feel they need to avoid me. I want to be able to say hi, shake hands, give them a hug, and wish them well. I believe that if you're a leader, that should also be your goal.

I think a lot of relationships are worth saving, but many can't be saved. I think we have to be realistic about the relationship, and do our best, but sometimes we have to accept that it can't be saved. We have to learn to say to ourselves, *It's OK. I don't have to keep this close relationship with this person anymore.* You have to be secure in your leadership and give yourself permission to have a different relationship from what you had before. You still value the person, but you let them go.

Questions Related to Working Under Poor Leadership

1. How can you succeed with a leader who is difficult to work with?

2. How would you work with a difficult leader who doesn't like you?

3. How would you work with a difficult leader who lacks vision?

4. How would you work with a difficult leader who is indecisive and inconsistent?

5. How would you work with a difficult leader who has attitude and character problems?

6. How would you work with a difficult leader who acts like a bully?

7. How would you work with a difficult leader who always plays it safe?

8. If someone who had a higher position than you did not have good leadership skills, how would you go about running the organization in a respectful way?

8

How Can I Succeed Working Under Poor Leadership?

In thirty years of teaching leadership conferences, I've heard one question more than any other. How do I work with a bad leader? People struggle working for those who aren't any good as leaders, or working with leaders less talented than they are. It's a source of endless frustration. Everything rises and falls on leadership. If you work for a bad leader, you probably feel like it mostly falls...on you!

In this chapter I discuss this issue. I give a strategy for finding success when dealing with a leader who's difficult to work with. My assumption going in is that you've already tried to be cooperative and work things out with him or her. The process I share is designed to force the issue. And I'll be very candid with you. Sometimes it works. Sometimes it doesn't. You have no control over that. You can only control what you do, and how you respond. Wayne W. Dyer says, "How people treat you is their karma. How you react is yours."

> "How people treat you is their karma. How you react is yours."
> —*Wayne W. Dyer*

If everything goes well, you've made a tremendous breakthrough. If things don't go the way you hoped or planned, it may be time to move on. If you decide to stay and try to make the best of the situation, I provide a few strategies for the most common problems related to difficult leaders. You'll find those later in this chapter.

I believe leaders are responsible for who and what they lead. Bad bosses often shirk their responsibilities and try to place them on the follower—on you—and you end up carrying the load. Whenever this happens, as far as it's possible, you should attempt to ask questions of your leader in such a way that the responsibility goes back on his or her shoulders where it belongs.

1. How Can You Succeed with a Leader Who Is Difficult to Work With?

There are as many kinds of bad leaders as there are kinds of people in the world, and they create many different kinds of difficulty. But the outcome of their leadership is always the same. The people under them suffer and so does the organization.

Though each problem is unique, the process for trying to reach a positive solution is similar in nearly all circumstances. If you are working for a bad or difficult leader, and you intend to try to improve the situation, you need to do your homework and go through a deliberate process to seek resolution. This will increase your chances for a positive outcome. However, you need to go into the process with realistic expectations. Many poor leaders do not respond well to having their methods questioned. So part of what you will be doing is preparing yourself for what you will do if it doesn't go well.

That doesn't mean you should shrink from the task, especially if interaction with your leader is causing a violation of your values, the erosion of your confidence, or the undermining of your ability to achieve success in your work. You need to move forward. Here is how I suggest you proceed:

1. Consider Whether *You* Might Actually Be the Problem

It's often easy to point out all the things that someone else is doing wrong, but when we do that, we sometimes neglect to examine ourselves to see what *we* are doing wrong. As I've mentioned before, the number one challenge I face as a leader is leading myself.

Someone once said, "Open minds lead to open doors." If I want to try to solve a problem with someone else, I need to first own up to my part in it and work to fix it. So before you start looking at what's wrong with your leader, first determine what's wrong with you.

2. Determine Whether You Have Specific Evidence to Support Your Opinion

Statesman-philanthropist Bernard Baruch said, "Every man has a right to his opinion, but no man has a right to be wrong in his facts." Before you decide to meet with your leader, you need to be sure the conflict or problem you see is based on solid evidence—not merely your feelings, not hearsay from someone else, not conjecture. Exactly what actions has your leader taken that are wrong? What specific words did you hear your leader say that were offensive or derogatory? Be specific. If you can't be specific, you may be wrong in your assessment of the situation.

Even if you can cite specifics, try to examine them rationally, without emotion. The great Roman orator Cicero observed, "So near is the line between falsehood and truth that a wise man would do well not to trust himself on the narrow edge."

Why It's Important to Be Specific

The higher the stakes, the more important it is that you have solid, specific evidence.

- The more important the message, the more important it is to give evidence.
- The more important the person, the more important it is to give evidence.
- The more important the timing, the more important it is to give evidence.

---

3. Assess Your Influence and Credibility with Your Leader

You can be right and have all your facts lined up, but if you have no influence with your leader, you may not get anywhere. Credibility opens the door to communication, and its lack closes it. As Neil Postman observed, "The credibility of the teller is the ultimate test of the truth of a proposition." So even if what you say is correct, if you have little credibility in the eyes of your leader, the perception may be that your observations have no truth.

> "The credibility of the teller is the ultimate test of the truth of a proposition."
> —Neil Postman

For that reason, before you try to do anything to address the issue, you need to figure out where you stand with him or her. What kind of clout do you have? Hotel executive Maria Razumich-Zec says, "Your reputation and integrity are everything. Follow through on what you say you're going to do. Your credibility can only be built over time, and it is built from the history of your words and actions."

If you're not sure where you stand, talk to your coworkers. Ask them how much weight they think your words carry with the boss. If you have some degree of credibility, your leader might be willing to listen when you have difficult or negative things to say.

4. Think Through Every Possible Outcome

When most people are unhappy with their leader and their situation at work, they go to their coworkers to complain. By planning to talk to your leader instead, you are trying to do the right thing. But you should have the discussion with your leader only if you are willing to accept the outcome. That means you need to take the time to think about all the different responses your leader might give you and determine what you would do in every instance.

Author and philosopher Brand Blanshard shared his steps for thinking through a problem. You might want to try them:

> The first step is to make the problem specific. The second step is to form theories freely of how to rid yourself of that burden. The third step is to develop in foresight the consequences of your proposals. The fourth and final step is to compare the consequences of your proposals to see which is best in the light of your scheme in life as a whole. Whether you choose a vacation or a spouse, a party or a candidate, a cause to contribute to or a creed to live by—think!

Blanshard's steps assume that you will be making all the decisions, which won't be true in your case. You will have no control over how your leader reacts. President Abraham Lincoln said, "When I am getting ready to reason with a man, I spend one-third of my time thinking about myself and what I am going to say—and two-thirds thinking about him and what he is going to say." That's probably a good rule of thumb. If you put in the time, think things through, anticipate the possible reactions of your leader, and know what you will do in any given situation, you are as prepared as you can be.

5. Make a Decision to Act

At this point you have a decision to make. To do things the right way, you need to either take action or accept your situation as it is. If you decide not to take action, move on and don't say anything negative to others about your situation. Never complain about what you allow. If you do, that puts *you* in the wrong. If you are in a situation that's bad for you, you need to act. Just remember, as Jules Ellinger said, "There has never been a statue erected to the memory of someone who left well enough alone."

> **"There has never been a statue erected to the memory of someone who left well enough alone."**
> —*Jules Ellinger*

6. Ask to Speak with Your Leader Privately

One of the worst mistakes you can make with difficult leaders is to criticize them or call them out publicly. That always turns into a lose-lose proposition. Just as you would hope that your leader would take you aside to share criticism, you should do the same with him or her.

7. Meet, Outline Your Complaint, and Seek a Collaborative Solution

When you meet with your leader, your goal should not be to vent or get even. The point is not to complain. The point is to seek a positive resolution. Present your evidence in a way that is as positive, non-threatening, and non-accusatory as possible. Explain why you find it difficult to work and get your job done, and ask if there is anything that you and your leader can do to resolve the situation and work together more positively.

If you are honest, yet treat your leader with respect, at the end of the discussion you can walk away from the meeting with your integrity intact, no matter what the outcome is. Hopefully you and your leader will be able to agree upon a course of action that will serve both of you well. If your leader refuses to accept responsibility, becomes defensive, or proposes something you're not sure you can agree to, ask for time to think it over. You can always meet again later to try again for a positive solution. If he or she suggests something that you know is good and right, that's great. Move forward with it. As pioneer automaker Henry Ford said, "If everyone is moving forward together, then success takes care of itself."

8. Determine Whether You Should Stay or It's Time to Move On

You will have to make a decision after you meet with your leader. Will you stay or will you go? Maybe your leader says he will change. If that turns out to be true, great. Maybe he says he will not change. Are you willing to live with that? Maybe the conversation you had with your leader did greater damage to the relationship. As someone once said, "Relationships are like glass. Sometimes it is better to leave them broken than to hurt yourself trying to put them back together." In the end you may not be able to change the people around you, but you can change the people you choose to be around.

If you're still having a hard time trying to decide whether to stay or go, ask yourself this question: if I weren't already working here, knowing what I know now, would I want to become part of this organization? If the answer is no, it's time to go. If the answer is "I don't know," ask yourself again in six months. If the answer is yes, stay and learn how to work with your leader.

9. If You Decide You Can Stay, Give Your Best and Publicly Support Your Leader

If you think that you might want to stay and keep working with your leader, you need to ask yourself two crucial questions:

Will I be able to add value?
Will I be able to stay true to myself?

If you cannot answer yes to both of those questions, it would be better for you to leave. But if you can add value and stay true to yourself, you need to publicly support your leader. Stay quiet about the negative things you know about him or her. When you're tempted to say something negative, say something nice instead. And if you need to discuss a problem or address a difficulty, do it behind closed doors. You should never do anything that compromises your integrity, but you need to remain supportive after the discussion. NFL coach Vince Lombardi pointed out, "Individual commitment to a group effort is what makes a team work, a company work, a civilization work." If you're not supporting the team with your individual effort, you're hurting the team.

For most of my career, I was the top leader in an organization. That didn't always mean I was the greatest influencer, but it did mean that I didn't have a positional boss directing me in my work. The churches belonged to a larger entity, a denomination, but the local churches I led were pretty autonomous.

About ten years into my career, I wanted to make a greater impact on more leaders, so I decided to leave the local church I was leading and work for the denomination at its headquarters. In the corporate world, that's like a person who owns a restaurant franchise selling his restaurant and going to work for the parent corporation.

I did it because I wanted to train and affect leaders beyond my own local church, and I thought this was the best way to do it. What I hadn't realized was that I would feel restricted working in just one denomination. And I was reporting to someone who wasn't a good leader. He thought like a manager or bureaucrat, not an entrepreneur or leader. It was not a good fit for me, and I realized it pretty quickly.

I spent most of my time out in the field training leaders, but I still had to answer to this leader, and we were on totally different pages most of the time. So I made an appointment to meet with him and discuss the issues. After the meeting, I realized my time there needed to come to an end. Having him as my direct leader wasn't going to work.

I worked in that position for eighteen months. After realizing I needed to make a change, whenever there was a problem, I went to him privately to discuss it, and I tried to work with him as much as I could. Meanwhile I looked for the right opportunity elsewhere. But I never criticized him to others. In fact, in the thirty-five years since I left, this is the first time I've talked about it publicly.

2. How Would You Work with a Difficult Leader Who Doesn't Like You?

It's difficult to work with someone you think doesn't like you, especially when it's your leader. Most people don't respond to it well. They often do one of the following:

• **Hide from the person:** Many people go into avoidance mode. The good news is that there isn't direct conflict. The bad news is that when we spend our energy hiding, we lose momentum.

• **Hinder the person:** Another common response is to become passive-aggressive. We don't do anything directly destructive. We just make sure not to be very cooperative. The problem with this is it hurts the team and causes us to be unfocused.

• **Harm the person:** The worst of all responses is to try to punish or harm the person who doesn't like us. That causes us to lose integrity.

Instead you need to take the high road. You cannot control your leader's response to you. He or she may never love working with you. But you can do everything in your power to make sure that you are not the cause of the problem. You do that by...

Processing Your Emotions

Over time, if your negative emotions are left unchecked and allowed to brew, they will overflow into every area of your working—and maybe also your private—life. These negative emotions can influence our decision making, taint how we view relationships, and affect how we lead our people. For that reason we need to feel our emotions regularly. We must acknowledge how we feel, work through any hurt feelings, and move on. Otherwise we're likely to hold a grudge.

Looking for Common Ground

Everyone sees the world from their own unique perspective. Terry Felber, author of *Am I Making Myself Clear?* wrote, "If you can learn to pinpoint how those around you experience the world, and really try to experience the same world they do, you'll be amazed at how effective your communication will become."

Whenever and wherever possible, look for points of agreement with your leader. And when you find them, focus on those things you have in common rather than the differences that set you apart. If you are united in a common goal, start there.

Being Consistently Pleasant

Noted English hostess Lady Dorothy Nevill observed, "The real art of conversation is not only to say the right thing at the right place, but to leave unsaid the wrong thing at the tempting moment." That means being consistently pleasant all the time.

Have you ever heard the phrase "Kill them with kindness"? People often soften if you stay constant when they are not—when you are sincere, kind, helpful, and pleasant despite their choices and behavior. And remember, as poet Kahlil Gibran asserted, "Tenderness and kindness are not signs of weakness and despair, but manifestations of strength and resolution."

> "Tenderness and kindness are not signs of weakness and despair, but manifestations of strength and resolution."
> —*Kahlil Gibran*

Solving Problems

One of the best ways to endear yourself to a leader is to be a good problem solver. It's easy to see and point out problems. It's much more difficult—and valuable—to offer and implement solutions. Adding value to others always works to your advantage. If you increase your value by becoming good at offering and implementing solutions, it will make your boss's job easier, and his or her attitude toward you might soften.

Going the Extra Mile

Film director William C. de Mille quipped, "I have always admired the ability to bite off more than one can chew, and then chew it." If you want to please people, go above and beyond expectations. Most of the differences between average and top people can be explained in three words: "and then some." If you do your job and then some, people will be drawn to you, maybe even your boss.

Sometimes people dislike another person without good reasons. That could be the case with you and your leader. All you can do is try to connect on common ground and be a great employee. It's difficult to dislike someone who consistently treats people with kindness, does the job well, and goes above and beyond what is expected. If you do all those things and your leader still doesn't like you, you can take comfort in knowing that you are probably not the cause of the problem.

3. How Would You Work with a Difficult Leader Who Lacks Vision?

CEO coach Mike Myatt says, "After character, the ability to create, articulate, evangelize, and execute on your vision is what will make or break you as a leader." That's why it's so difficult to work with a leader who lacks vision. Much dissatisfaction and discouragement are caused by absence of vision. Without it, leaders lack the ability to convey motivation, drive, and purpose to their people.

If you are going to stay and work under a leader who lacks vision, what can you do?

Tap into the Organization's Larger Vision

If you work for a larger organization in which your boss is only one leader of many, you can tap into the vision of the organization itself. When the vision of the organization is clear, the vision of any individual leader, team, or department within the organization should contribute to that larger vision anyway. It should work within that context.

How does your team or department support that larger vision of the organization? In what way does your team or department add the most value? How can you advance the purpose of the organization in a significant way? How can you make it better?

Identify a Vision for the Organization and Share It with Your Leader

If you work in a smaller organization where your leader is the top leader, you may want to work at discovering and developing a vision for the organization that will help it succeed. Once you've done that, you can share it with your leader, and if your level of influence is strong, your leader might embrace it and buy into it.

If you do this, just be sure that the vision is consistent with the values and goals you know your leader possesses. If it's not, your leader will probably not welcome it.

Develop Your Own Sense of Purpose

Scottish philosopher Thomas Carlyle asserted, "A person with a clear purpose will make progress on even the roughest road. A person with no purpose will make no progress on even the smoothest road." What a great image. Purpose gives you drive. It shows you a destination. It paints a picture of your future. It energizes you. And it makes obstacles and problems seem small in comparison to its importance.

You cannot allow your leader's lack of vision to keep you from making progress in life. Connect with and develop your own purpose. As long as you are doing work consistent with it, you won't be as bothered by your leader's lack of vision for the organization. You will just need to be certain that you are doing what you were created to do.

To Discover Your Own Sense of Purpose...

Listen to the inner voice: This is where you receive your mission.
Listen to the unhappy voice: This is where you receive your ideas.
Listen to the successful voice: This is where you receive your advice.
Listen to the customer's voice: This is where you receive your feedback.
Listen to the higher voice: This is where you receive your attitude.

Vision is critical to good leadership. I have yet to meet a great leader who lacks vision. In discussing CEOs, Mike Myatt says,

> Leaders without vision will fail. Leaders who lack vision cannot inspire teams, motivate performance, or create sustainable value. Poor vision, tunnel vision, vision that is fickle, or a non-existent vision will cause leaders to fail. A leader's job is to align the organization around a clear and achievable vision. This cannot occur when the blind lead the blind."[27]

I absolutely agree that any organization whose top organization lacks vision is in trouble. Farther down the leadership chain, is it ideal to have leaders without vision? No. But it is possible for someone to lead up in the organization to influence a leader without vision. It isn't easy, but it is possible.

4. How Would You Work with a Difficult Leader Who Is Indecisive and Inconsistent?

Psychologist William James said, "There is no more miserable human being than one in whom nothing is habitual but indecision." I might have to disagree with that. I believe the people who have that indecisive human being as their leader and have to work for him are at least equally miserable.

Leaders who cannot make decisions are like lobsters, according to author and physician Orison Swett Marden. He wrote,

> A lobster, when left high and dry among the rock, does not have the sense enough to work his way back to the sea, but waits for the sea to come to him. If it does not come, he remains where he is and dies, although the slightest effort would enable him to reach the waves, which are perhaps within a yard of him. The world is full of human lobsters; people stranded on the rocks of indecision and procrastination, who, instead of putting forth their own energies are waiting for some grand billow of good fortune to set them afloat.

If you can see solutions within arm's reach, yet your leader prevents you from implementing them, you will be continually frustrated. What can you do to deal with this situation?

Ask Permission to Make the Decisions

Leadership decisions should always be made at the lowest possible level. The people on the front lines usually know the problems and solutions best. They are also closest to the problems and can usually act quickly. So if you know what decisions should be made, ask your leaders if they are willing to let you make them. If they seem unsure, offer to start small with minor decisions that won't make or break the team. In that way you can develop credibility and a positive track record. If they say yes and you're willing to

> Leadership decisions should always be made at the lowest possible level.

take responsibility for your own decisions and actions, the problem is solved.

Offer to Help Your Leaders Process Decisions

If you are good at decision making and can see solutions readily, but your leaders don't want to release you to act independently, offer to privately process decisions with them. Gather information and present it to them. Define each problem as specifically as you can. Offer a variety of solutions, taking into account their values, motivations, priorities, and goals. Explain the implications of every decision as you see them. Then ask for a decision.

If they are unwilling to come to a conclusion, ask for feedback. Try to find which solutions they prefer and which they dismiss out of hand. In this way you can find out how they think and try to narrow down the options. If they still won't make a decision, try to get them to commit to a deadline. Then circle back later to try to land the decision.

Ask What You Are to Do When a Decision *Must* Be Made

If you have leaders who will not allow you to either make the decisions or help them make them, your only course of action is to be very direct with them and privately ask the question, "What do you want me to do when a decision *must* be made but you aren't making it?" Likewise, if you work with inconsistent leaders, you must ask a similar question when they change their minds: "Previously you decided that; how do you want me to proceed now that you've decided this?"

By asking these questions, you are putting the ball back in your leaders' court where it belongs. They are the ones responsible for making decisions. But if they don't take responsibility, at least you have a course of action that they have asked you to take in those situations, and when they change their minds again, you can say with integrity, "The last time we talked, you said you wanted me to do this, and that's what I've done."

5. How Would You Work with a Difficult Leader Who Has Attitude and Character Problems?

One of the great dangers in working for leaders who have attitude and character problems is that they are continually trying to drag you down to wherever they are. Bad attitudes are contagious. It's difficult to remain positive when people around you are continually negative. And people who cheat or cut corners in their lives will inevitably ask you to do the same, and they won't want to take no for an answer when you refuse to share their methods.

Leaders with these kinds of issues are like crabs in a bucket. If you've ever caught crabs or seen someone else do it, you know that if you toss two crabs in a bucket, you never have to worry about either one of them getting away from you. The crabs are so focused on dragging one another down that they never think of getting out of the bucket themselves. That's the way it will probably feel to you in that environment. It will be a constant struggle for you to retain a positive attitude and maintain your values.

If you are determined to stay in such an environment, the best thing you can try to do is lift people to a higher level. Here's how you can do that:

Live on a Higher Level Yourself

You don't want to allow others' compromises to influence you to compromise your own values. But that alone is not enough. One of your goals as a leader and person should always be to be a positive influence on others in the critical areas of attitude and character. If your leaders aren't strong in these areas, try to lead up and help them as well as your peers and those you lead.

The way to start doing that is by holding yourself to the highest possible standard. You cannot take people where you haven't been. As you gain a reputation for being positive and reliable by maintaining high standards for yourself, your credibility will increase, and so will your influence. You may have opportunities to help others realize there's a better way to do things and to make better choices.

Separate Yourself from Negative Influences as Much as Possible

Trying to help others to be positive and honest using influence alone doesn't always work. People have been given free will and make their own choices in life. If you've done your best to help your leaders but you start to feel their influence negatively affecting your attitude or values, separate yourself from them as much as you can. If time and distance don't seem to be helping, consider leaving your position. No job is worth trading your integrity for.

Put Things in Writing Whenever Possible

To a great extent you can avoid a bad attitude. However, you need to protect yourself from someone who has no integrity. As I've already discussed, the best way to do that is to leave so you don't become party to anything unethical. But if you can't leave right away or if you need to stay for some reason, put as much communication as you can in writing. You will want to be able to show evidence of your right-doing if at some point your boss is accused of wrongdoing.

6. How Would You Work with a Difficult Leader Who Acts Like a Bully?

I read in *Forbes* that a 2010 survey conducted by the Workplace Bullying Institute reports that 35 percent of the American work force has experienced "repeated mistreatment by one or more employees that takes the form of verbal abuse, threats, intimidation, humiliation, or sabotage of work performance." Approximately 72 percent of those bullies are bosses.[28] That's a huge number, and it's an indication that many people who hold leadership positions or titles don't understand how good leadership works. It's based on invitation, not intimidation.

Having bosses who act like bullies makes life difficult. Nobody likes to feel pushed around. If you decide to stay in such an environment, your best bet is to try to let what they say roll off you like water off a duck's back. Don't buy into what they're selling. That's not going to be easy, so here are some suggestions to help you:

1. Be Confident in Your Own Value

Former first lady Eleanor Roosevelt said, "No one can make you feel inferior without your consent." Leaders cannot devalue you without your permission. Unpleasant bosses can say anything they want to you or about you, but if it isn't true, you don't need to buy into it. You prevent that by seeing the value in yourself and being confident in it.

> "No one can make you feel inferior without your consent."
> —*Eleanor Roosevelt*

You have value. Every person does. You have talents and skills that can add value to others. You have resources and opportunities that no one else has. You have intrinsic value simply because you are a human being. You need to own these things. Philosopher-poet Ralph

Waldo Emerson said, "Make the most of yourself, for that is all there is of you."

Even if you do everything right, there's no guarantee that others won't treat you wrong. People can decide they don't like you with no legitimate reason. You can't control that. Instead be confident and think of the words of Winston Churchill, who was prime minister of Great Britain during World War II: "You have enemies? Good. That means you've stood up for something, sometime in your life." Develop thick skin, and your critics won't bother you as much.

2. Do Not Accept Blame That Doesn't Belong to You

Author and lecturer John Killinger tells a story about a baseball manager for a minor-league team who was frustrated by the poor play of his center fielder. Finally, in disgust, he marched into center field, told the player he was out of the game, and took his place himself.

The first ball that came his way took a bad hop and hit him in the mouth. The next was a high fly ball, which he lost in the sun. It hit him in the forehead. The third ball was a sharp line drive that he charged, arms stretched forward to catch it; he stumbled and the ball hit him in the eye.

When the inning was finally over, he ran to the dugout, grabbed his center fielder by the uniform, and shouted, "You idiot! You've got center field so messed up that even I can't do a thing with it!"

Bullies are always looking for someone to blame. Don't allow them to blame you for things you're not responsible for. If something is your fault, own up to it. If it's not, decline to take the blame.

3. Refuse to Be a Victim

One of the reasons some people allow themselves to be bullied is that they feel powerless to do anything about what's happening to them; they believe that they're victims. It's important for you not to allow yourself to think that way. You can't develop a victim's mind-set and be successful.

First lady Michelle Obama explained, "One of the lessons that I grew up with was to always stay true to yourself and never let what somebody else says distract you from your goals. And so when I hear about negative and false attacks, I really don't invest any energy in them, because I know who I am."

If you know who you are and you take a proactive approach to life, you are less likely to feel like a victim. You can't do everything, but you can do some things. You can't prevent others from treating you poorly, but you can decide how you will respond.

Albert Ellis asserted, "By not caring too much about what people think, I'm able to think for myself and propagate ideas which are very often unpopular. And I succeed." That is your goal.

7. How Would You Work with a Difficult Leader Who Always Plays It Safe?

Management expert Peter Drucker said, "It's easier for companies to come up with new ideas than to let go of old ones." Why is that? Fear. Many people are afraid of change, of risk, of failure. They don't want to let go of the known because they fear the unknown.

I once saw an article in the *Saturday Evening Post* that talked about fear. It said that many people fear dying in a plane crash, yet the odds against that happening are 250,000 to one. A person is more likely to be kicked to death by a donkey than to die in a plane crash. People are also afraid of being murdered, yet a person is eight times more likely to die while playing a sport than to be shot by a stranger. People fear dying on the operating table during surgery, yet they are twenty times more likely to die in an automobile accident. At the same time, millions of people hope and pray they will win the lottery. The truth is that they are three times more likely to be struck by lightning.

People's fears and worries are often overblown. Many times they're not based in reality. Yet these worries stop them from being productive and successful just the same. If you have leaders who always play it safe, you may be able to help them. Try doing the following:

Put Yourself in Their Shoes

The story goes that when Michael Faraday invented the first electric motor, he wanted the interest and backing of the British prime minister, William Gladstone. So Faraday took a simple model comprised of a little wire revolving around a magnet to the statesman and showed it to him. Gladstone showed little interest and asked, "What good is it?"

Thinking quickly, the inventor responded, "Someday you will be able to tax it." Faraday didn't try to explain the device. He didn't try to persuade Gladstone. He simply put himself in his questioner's shoes. And it paid off. He received the backing he desired.

If you want to try to put yourself into your leaders' shoes, ask yourself three questions:

• **Where have they been?** This relates to their experiences. What is their background? What have they done in the past? What kinds of things have happened to them that may be causing them to be afraid of change?

• **What do they feel?** This relates to their emotions. Most people who won't take risks are afraid. Try to find out not only how they feel but how they process their emotions and deal with things like stress.

• **What do they want?** This relates to expectations. What really matters to them in life? What are their hopes and dreams? My friend Zig Ziglar said, "You can get anything in life you want, if you help enough people get what they want." If you know what they want and help them get it, maybe you'll get what you want too.

Sales expert Tom Hopkins, who wrote *How to Master the Art of Selling*, advises that if you want to close a deal, you must see through the eyes of the client. The same is true when you're working for weak leaders. If you want to understand them and work *with* them, you must see things from their perspective. That's the best way to help them and yourself.

Acknowledge Their Feelings

Leaders who avoid risk do so generally because they do not have the confidence to believe in their own success. Don't dismiss those feelings of fear and inadequacy. Instead acknowledge them. And as far as you are able, help them to achieve small wins. This can help them build their confidence.

Help Them Take Action

Sometimes what people need are facts. They need to see the greater value of a specific change. Yes, all of us can be hurt. All of us can and at times will fail. But progress always takes risk. Help your leaders weigh the potential gains and losses of taking action against the potential gains and losses of not taking it. If you can take the worst, take the risk. As General George S. Patton said, "A good plan vigorously executed right now is far better than a perfect plan executed next week."

8. If Someone Who Had a Higher Position than You Did Not Have Good Leadership Skills, How Would You Go About Running the Organization in a Respectful Way?

Often people who work for bosses with poor leadership skills try to fight the situation. That's an approach that is not likely to work. Instead they need to try to help their bosses to succeed, because if *we* want to be successful, we must try to help others to succeed. We can't undermine our leaders and expect our team to be successful. And if they're smart, they will understand that they cannot make it without us. We need each other.

1. Understand Your Leader

When people have asked me about working for poor leaders, I often find that they don't really know those leaders. They are so preoccupied by what their leaders aren't doing right that they don't even try to find out who they are. That's a mistake. To help yourself, you need to help them. To help them, you need to know what they care about.

Ask Your Leader...

- **What is your heart?** These are the things your leaders care about. As far as it's within your power, provide them.
- **What is your hope?** These are the things your leaders want to do. As far as they align with your values, promote them.
- **What causes you hurt?** These are the things your leaders want to avoid. As far as you're able, protect your leaders from them.
- **How can I help?** There are many things your leaders want to do but cannot do alone. Your task is to partner with them to get those things done.

As you get to know your leaders and endeavor to help them, you will start to look at them as people first and leaders second. Your communication with them will improve. So will your connection. You may even begin to enjoy working together.

When we do our own work and follow through successfully in our assignments, we place ourselves in a position for promotion. When we contribute to the success of our bosses, they are put in a position to rise. As they do, guess whom they want to bring along with them? The people who help them win. As John Mason says, "Making others better is a boomerang."

2. Understand Your Support Role

Although your leadership skills may be greater than those of the people you work for, if you want to be successful, you have to play your part. You've been hired to play a supporting role. Do your best to fulfill it with excellence.

3. Bloom Where You're Planted

Few things impress leaders, whether they are strong or weak, like a worker who is both a starter and a finisher. If you have initiative and are a self-starter, doing your work with joy, everyone will want to work with you. If you follow through on tasks and commitments, people will give you greater and greater responsibilities. The measure of a person is not what he or she says in the staff meeting, but rather what he or she does when the meeting is over.

4. Rise Above Others with a Right Attitude

It's hard for most people who work for weak leaders to maintain a great attitude. If you can be positive and supportive while all those around you are negative or complain, you will stand out and people will be drawn to you. Remember, good employees aren't people with a certain set of circumstances; they are people with a certain set of attitudes.

5. Succeed on Their Terms

When you're working in the middle of an organization with leaders above you, your success usually takes place on someone else's terms. You are not in charge of the definition of success. You cannot rewrite the rules of the game. The pathway to success has been set by others. The only thing you can do is succeed on the terms of others. This idea may frustrate you, but the reality is that everyone is accountable to someone and must succeed on others' terms.

> Life's greatest rewards come from your inner self, from the choices you make, from how you decide to live under whatever circumstances you find yourself in.

In the end, the only thing you can do is lead your life. If you don't, others will, by determining what will happen to you. Life's greatest rewards come from your inner self, from the choices you make, from how you decide to live under whatever circumstances you find yourself in.

Questions Related to Navigating Leadership Transitions

1. When is the right time for a successful leader to move on to a new position?

2. What steps can a leader take to implement the changes that an organization needs to be successful but resists making?

3. How do I change my mind-set from that of a producer to that of a leader?

4. As an entrepreneurial leader of a fast-growing organization, how do I know whether to transition my role to create structure and stability, or to hire leaders to fulfill the new needs?

5. What leadership principles enable a failed leader to lead again successfully?

6. Why do some leaders fail to have a successor?

7. What are the most important things a leader transitioning out of a position can do to ensure the success of the person taking over the role?

8. How do you handle leaving and breaking the news to a great team of great people who came to a company because you asked them to?

9. What should be the legacy of a successful leader?

9

How Can I Successfully Navigate Leadership Transitions?

We live in an age of change. It's said that in this decade, it takes only two days for people to create the amount of new information that it took all of civilization to create from the dawn of time up until 2003.[29]

And some experts estimate that most American workers today will change jobs between fifteen and twenty times in a career.[30] The days are long gone of finding a job and staying in it until you receive a gold watch and a pension.

Life means transition. Most people intuitively understand that the world is moving fast, yet they still have a difficult time with it. Brian Tracy was right when he said, "In a time of rapid change, standing still is the most dangerous course of action." If you don't learn how to make good transitions, you either get run over or get left behind.

One of the characteristics of good leaders is their ability to navigate transitions. That has always been true. They are able to make smooth transitions themselves. And they are also able to help their team members and their organizations do the same. The questions in this chapter will help you to become better at facing—and winning through—transition.

1. When Is the Right Time for a Successful Leader to Move On to a New Position?

Leaders often get restless. When they do, they start exploring opportunities and new mountains to climb. The more entrepreneurial the leaders, the shorter their attention spans often are. The key to knowing whether it's time to transition is recognizing that there are two kinds of restlessness: good and bad.

Good restlessness is healthy. It pulls you forward toward improvement. It comes from your desire to grow, to make a greater impact, to serve others more effectively. Every major growth decision I've made in life grew out of this positive kind of restlessness. It came when I thought to myself, *I can do better than this. There's more in me, and I want to tap into it.*

Bad restlessness comes from being bored or unhappy. It comes from a desire to escape. It causes you to be impatient. You often jump out of where you are, but not *to* anything specific. And as a result, it can actually put you in a worse place. I've seen many unsuccessful people allow this desire to escape drive them from place to place, and over the course of time, their situations actually declined. People experiencing the positive kind of restlessness are willing to hold steady until there's an opportunity to move to something better. As my friend Elmer Towns, co-founder of Liberty University, says, "Don't leave something; go to something."

> "Don't leave something; go to something."
> —*Elmer Towns*

There's one more thing to look at to determine whether the restlessness you feel is good or bad. Ask yourself whether you have given the best you have where you are now. Don't move anywhere else until you have.

Don't seek a move just to make things easier on yourself. To transition with integrity, you need to have done your best work possible. Then you can leave with a clear heart and mind. Besides, you always want to leave on a high note. If you're at the top of your game and you've given your best—you're at a peak—you can see farther than if you're in a valley.

Recognize What Kind of Restlessness You Are Experiencing

If you're feeling restless and desire to move on from your current position, role, or organization, ask yourself the following questions:

1. Do I desire to move *away* from something or *toward* something?
2. Have I given my very best where I am now?
3. Am I trying to get away from pain or go toward growth?
4. Am I willing to be patient and wait until a fantastic opportunity presents itself?

Once you're certain that your desire to transition is motivated by the right reasons, use the following steps to help you move through the process the right way.

1. Consider Your Possibilities

Every transition in life is a trade-off. Even when you leave a negative place, you leave behind some good things. Even if you go to a great place in your new role, there will be some things about it that you won't like. It's not black and white. And the more successful you are, the harder it is to make trade-offs, because you give up more when you trade off and transition. That's why some people become successful and then become flat.

As I've already explained, if you're experiencing the right kind of restlessness, you won't be driven to jump quickly to something else. Patience and maturity will empower you to consider your possibilities as you seek to transition. During that time, study, reflect, pray, plan, read, and write. Look for opportunities. Interview people who are ahead of you in the journey. Use the time to your advantage.

2. Weigh the Risks and Rewards

If you are patient and keep your eyes open, you will find an opportunity. Before you make a transition, it is wise to do a risk assessment. Sometimes when I do this I actually sit down with my legal pad and create two columns, one labeled "Risk" and the other "Reward." Then I list every risk and reward I can think of in the columns and compare the two. It's not just a matter of which list is longer. Not all entries are equal. A single risk or reward may carry so much weight that it tips the balance.

As you weigh the risks against the rewards, be sure to take into account things that tap into your passion, giving them extra weight. And ask yourself these questions:

• **Are the potential rewards greater than the risks?** Be as specific as you can about the rewards. You don't want to take a giant leap for a small reward or risk a lot for the potential of a small gain.

• **Is what you hope to do achievable?** There are no guarantees in life. You may not be certain about your ability to achieve what you desire. But you must know it's *possible* to achieve it.

• **Can you recover from the downside?** You need to know what the downsides are, and know that if the outcome is a disaster you will be able to recover from it. It's OK to fail. It's not smart to fail in a way you can't recover from.

It's generally not wise to transition without having clarity about where you want to go. You can follow your instinct, but you don't want to do it uninformed.

3. Receive Affirmation from Your Inner Circle

The most important person you need affirmation from when making a transition decision is yourself. You need to know your own heart. You need to have confidence. You don't want to make a move if you can't find peace within yourself. Otherwise you'll be plagued by doubt if something goes wrong. And that makes it hard for you to keep steady and persevere.

> The most important person you need affirmation from when making a transition decision is yourself.

Having said that, it's wise for you to get input from the people closest to you and from wise people ahead of you. I sought counsel from people for every major transition I've made. I sought advice for clarity, but not for confidence. The right people's opinions, thoughts, perspectives, and experience can provide a tremendous amount of clarity. They can clear things up for you quickly. Other people can help you see the bigger picture, especially when your head has been deep into the details. If your decision is right, their input should make that clearer to you.

4. Take Action and Move Forward

In the end, if you believe the decision to transition is right and you know where you desire to go, you need to take action. I've known many people who didn't make the leap when they thought they should, and who later regretted not having taken it. Most people I know who try, risk, and fail are satisfied because they had the courage to try. They have self-respect, even though they didn't get what they expected. Not everyone expects to get to the top, but everyone would like to have a shot at it.

Indecision and inaction are what hurt most people. Those who don't take the leap when they think they should, die slowly. They think about what might have been—especially as they get into their forties and fifties. Most decisions people regret in life are the ones they make that lead to inaction. If you're getting older, the only thing worse than not having made a decision when you were younger is not making it now if you still can. Don't live your life haunted by the question "What if?"

I have never had total clarity when it was time for me to make a change. I've never had a vision in which it was all laid out for me. My need for a transition has always come as I began feeling dissatisfied and thinking about other possibilities. When I'm in the right place doing the right thing, I don't think of any other possibilities. I just love what I'm doing and can't imagine doing anything else. I'm excited and I want everyone around me to be excited. I want them to have a chance to get involved and benefit from what's happening. When I start to feel some dissatisfaction, it's often because I can't grow any more and my current situation is limiting my potential. That's when I start to open myself up to other possibilities and move from an intuitive sense of a transition to the more concrete process I've described.

2. What Steps Can a Leader Take to Implement the Changes that an Organization Needs to Be Successful but Resists Making?

Former US president Woodrow Wilson said, "If you want to make enemies, change something." Few people like change and welcome it. I used to think that leaders liked change and followers didn't, but the truth is that leaders don't like it any more than anyone else does—unless it was their idea!

> "If you want to make enemies, change something."
> —Woodrow Wilson

All change does not represent progress, but without change there can be no progress. And it is often up to leaders to initiate and implement changes. But here's the good news: if people need change, they often look to leaders for inspiration and guidance. Civil rights leader Martin Luther King Jr. observed, "People are often led to causes and often become committed to great ideas through persons who personify those ideas. They have to find the embodiment of the idea in flesh and blood in order to commit themselves to it."

If you find yourself in a position where you are the leader who must lead the charge for change, keep in mind the following guidelines:

Change What Needs to Be Changed, Not What Is Easy to Change

When organizations are having difficulties, leaders instinctively know that changes need to be made. One question is whether they will make real needed changes or merely cosmetic ones. Cosmetic changes are relatively easy to make. They give the semblance of change, but often don't actually produce positive results.

Changes that can make a difference are harder. Changing organizational culture when it's unhealthy, for example, is difficult. So is changing values. Or leaders and the way they are developed. But these kinds of efforts are what really change an organization.

The second organization I led had plateaued before I arrived. In an effort to start making progress again, it made changes, but they were only cosmetic. It changed its name—a common strategy that brings little positive benefit if it's the only thing that's done. It made minor improvements to the facility. It changed meeting times. These things did not create growth.

What needed changing was the culture. As soon as I got there, I started developing and equipping leaders. That was a slow and difficult process. But it created lasting change. After a year the organization began to grow. It wasn't long before we started to plan the building of larger facilities.

As I write this, I'm currently working to facilitate a major change in one of my organizations, EQUIP. For over ten years we've been training leaders, and we've been very successful. EQUIP is the most successful leadership training organization in the world, having trained more than five million leaders in nearly every country in the world. But I believe EQUIP is capable of more. We are working to shift from training to transformation. We want to make a significant impact on people in the countries where EQUIP operates.

Will that mean easy change? No. Is there any guarantee we will succeed? No. But we are giving it our best because if we *do* succeed, we will help transform people's lives. And if you help enough people to transform, they will transform their nations.

Let Go of Yesterday So You Can Go to Tomorrow

Bill Gates, co-founder and former CEO of Microsoft, once said, "In three years every product my company makes will be obsolete. The only question is whether we will make it obsolete or someone else will." Because of the speed of change in technology today, people who work in that area accept that they must let go of yesterday and embrace change for the sake of tomorrow. Those of us who aren't technical or don't work in related industries seem to have a more difficult time with this concept.

Authors and consultants Eric Harvey and Steve Ventura assert, "Our brains are like closets. Over time they are filled with things that we no longer use—things that don't fit. Every once in a while they need to be cleaned out." If you are going to lead change, you need to clean out your closet, and you need to help the people you lead to do the same. That's often not just a practical or intellectual exercise; it's also an emotional one.

Acknowledge the importance of the past. Honor the people who have made past contributions. But also show them why they can't stay where they are, and why the place you want to take them is so much better.

Communicate the Message with Simplicity and Power

Good leaders take the complex and make it simple. That is a hall-mark of a good communicator. That's not easy, but who ever said lead-ership was supposed to be easy?

There is great power in a simple clear message. A really good example of a leader's power to communicate clearly comes from the leadership of Roberto Goizueta at the Coca-Cola Company in the 1980s. Goizueta was one of the most successful CEOs in Coke's his-tory and made Coca-Cola the most prominent trademark in the world. One of the things he often said to impress upon people the growth potential of Coke was this: each of the six billion people on this planet drinks, on average, sixty-four ounces of fluids daily, of which only two ounces are Coca-Cola. What a clear picture. Closing the "sixty-two gap" became a centerpiece of inspiration and motivation within the company. People embraced change in order to achieve it.

The other thing you need to do as you communicate the vision for change is to give people multiple reasons for it. The more reasons for change, the more likely people are to accept it. Certainly the main rea-son will probably be that it is better for the organization. But how is it also good for customers, clients, and the community? And how is it better for the people in the organization who must implement the change? Never underestimate the importance of answering the ques-tion "What's in it for me?"

Activate Belief in People

As you work to implement changes, you must believe in them. Without conviction you won't give yourself 100 percent to the changes. People will sense that and will not follow you. But believing in the cause is not enough. You must also believe in the people who will make the change. Without that conviction they will not move forward. Former General Electric CEO Jack Welch observed, "Any time there is change, there is opportunity. So it is paramount that an organization get energized rather than paralyzed."

You energize an organization by energizing its people. You activate their belief in themselves. Your confidence in them will give them confidence in themselves. As J. Sterling Livingston said, "People perform consistently as they perceive you expect them to perform."

Finding Barriers

It's easy to get used to barriers and begin thinking they are normal and don't need to be changed. You may need to shake up your thinking in order to move forward. Ask yourself:

1. What internal barriers do I need to remove personally to help facilitate needed changes?
2. What policies are antithetical to the needed changes and how can I remove them?
3. What unnecessary tasks can be eliminated to free people to implement the needed changes?
4. What resources can be freed up to help make the needed changes possible?
5. Who is trying to obstruct needed changes and how can I get those people to change?

Remove Barriers for People

Once you communicate the need and vision for change and help people to believe they *can* change, your most important task as a leader is to start removing barriers that will keep people from executing the plan. Barriers are usually created by outdated systems, complicated procedures, difficult people, or strained resources. To find the barriers, get out among the people, watch what they're doing, and listen to their complaints.

Lead with Speed

Speed is important in creating short-term wins. Never underestimate the significance of early victories for giving people confidence to keep moving forward. Wins nourish faith in the change effort. They give an emotional lift to the people who are carrying and implementing the change. And they silence critics. Every win helps to build momentum, which is a leader's best friend. As former college football coach Darrel Royal said, "Luck follows speed."

3. How Do I Change My Mind-Set from That of a Producer to That of a Leader?

Most of us get our first opportunity to lead because we are personally successful. We produce for the organization, and some leader in the organization wants us to help others do the same. When that happens, we need to shift our focus.

PRODUCER	LEADER
Concentrates on tasks	Concentrates on team
Feels indispensible in what they do	Feels responsible for what others do
Possesses tunnel vision	Possesses team vision
Thinks, "How can I help?"	Thinks, "Who can help us?"
Asks, "What can I do?"	Asks, "What can we do?"
Produces through addition	Produces through multiplication

Put simply, to shift from producer to leader, a person must make the mind shift from *me* to *we*.

If you're a good producer, you probably know how you personally contribute to the vision of the organization. Ask yourself, "How does this team contribute to the vision?" and "How can every individual member contribute to the team?" Your job is to maximize the team's effort to fulfill the vision.

You also need to work to build relationships with the people on your team. If you are naturally a task-oriented person, this may be a stretch. Get to know your team as individuals and try to connect with them. Look for ways to add value to them. Find ways to lift them up with encouragement and gratitude. You can't really know what everyone's best contribution is until you know everyone.

As a producer, you already know how to win. As a leader, your job is to help the entire team win. You know how to cross the finish line individually. Now find ways to rally and guide everyone on your team to cross the finish line together.

4. As an Entrepreneurial Leader of a Fast-Growing Organization, How Do I Know Whether to Transition My Role to Create Structure and Stability, or to Hire Leaders to Fulfill the New Needs?

Success in an organization often creates as great a need for change as lack of success. Many people don't recognize that. It's obvious that in an organization that's not succeeding, leaders need to create change to get forward progress and create momentum. However, when organizations are highly successful, especially smaller organizations, leaders must make changes to sustain success and increase momentum. If they rely too long on past successes and keep doing what they've always done, the organization will eventually hit a wall.

In small entrepreneurial organizations, the top leaders are often the catalysts for the organizations. They are the ones who see opportunities, produce organizational energy, and create synergy between the organization and its customers. Their passion and personalities have driven the organization's success. They've probably made most if not all of the key decisions. And they've been able to touch everything and everyone in the organization to keep it on track.

As the organization grows, they can't keep doing that. They see and feel the need for structure and processes. So the question is, do you change your role? Do you try to focus on creating stability and structure for the organization?

If you are the catalyst for your organization, my admonition is to not lose your strength. Small organizations are personality driven. The leader's passion drives everything, and the leader breathes fire into the people. In your need to solve problems or desire to grow, don't institutionalize your organization too quickly. Instead of changing your role, channel your energy. Here's how:

Invite Your Inner Circle to Help You Focus Your Energy

Most entrepreneurial leaders don't struggle to find opportunities. They struggle to focus on the best opportunities. And the more gifted the leaders, the greater the number of options available to them.

> Most entrepreneurial leaders don't struggle to find opportunities. They struggle to focus on the best opportunities.

There was about a decade in my leadership when I got bombarded with opportunities, but I wasn't always sure about which ones to pursue. I was still doing some fine-tuning of my leadership and communication, and there were a lot of different directions in which I could go. I solved the problem of focus by forming what I called the Hatchet Committee. It was comprised of several key leaders, along with my wife and my assistant. Once a month we met to review opportunities, discuss strategy, and weigh choices. They shared their perspectives, offered wisdom, and reminded me to stay in my strength zone even when I stepped out of my comfort zone. The organization and I benefited highly from their input.

If you decide to do something similar, make sure you have the right people in the room. They need to understand the importance of your entrepreneurial spirit and have the wisdom and skill to channel it, not control it or try to stop it for their own comfort or convenience. I also recommend that you meet fairly frequently. This is not a one-and-done kind of activity, especially in an entrepreneurial organization, where the landscape is constantly changing and you're continually reevaluating your opportunities. We met monthly. You may need to meet more frequently. Figure out what your rhythm should be.

Enlist People Who Maximize and Magnify Your Energy

Once you've narrowed your focus to the things that have the greatest potential, you need to make the most of them. One of the things I've always looked for in people on my team is the ability to maximize the opportunities we have.

For example, when my organization puts on an event at which I will speak, the amount of time I have to spend to personally prepare is the same whether I'm communicating to fifty people or five thousand. If my team can do the work to get more people in the room, it magnifies my energy and makes the most of it.

Every experience that involves other people can be magnified by those who understand the value of an opportunity, the importance of timing, the quality of the experience, and the impact of numbers. If you're the one who sees and seizes opportunities, bring around yourself leaders and support staff who can make the most of those opportunities.

Empower People Who Have Skill and Energy in Areas Where You Lack Them

I'm not big on structure. I think too many organizations over-emphasize it. And I think a lot of organizations use reorganization to try to solve problems when they don't know what else to do. Instead I prefer a leadership-driven model of organization. Put the right leaders into place, train and develop them well, then empower them to make an impact in their area.

Over the years I've been fortunate enough to employ good leaders who possess skills in areas where I'm lacking or have little patience. They have put into place structure and processes that have created stability for my organizations, but we're still entrepreneurial. The structure needs to serve the vision and the leadership, not the other way around.

As your organization grows, look for people who share your values and have a deep appreciation for opportunity and impact, but who can bring organizational skills to the table to help you build a framework that will further growth and serve the vision. The energy that you bring and that is already felt throughout the company will be even better when it's channeled correctly.

5. What Leadership Principles Enable a Failed Leader to Lead Again Successfully?

When leaders fail, whether the breakdown occurs as a result of poor character, bad judgment, or lack of skill, one of the first things they think about is often how to move back into leadership. I think that's only natural, because leaders love to lead. However, I think they err if they don't first stop and take time to correct whatever problems they've had. If they don't, they are very likely to keep repeating the same mistakes.

If you've failed as a leader and lost your position, you need to consider the following before attempting to return to leadership:

Evaluation: What Went Wrong?

Before you can move back into a leadership role, you need to fix whatever problems you have in your leadership. You can't do that if you don't know what they are. Where did you go wrong? Was it a mistake in strategy? Did you lack skills necessary for good leadership? Do your problems stem from poor self-leadership? The last is the most common issue for failed leaders, but it is often the most difficult for them to see on their own. If you're not sure what went wrong, talk to people with firsthand knowledge to get their perspective.

Emotional Strength: Can You Bounce Back?

I strongly believe that people need to learn how to fail forward, and I believe they can. However, it requires emotional strength. If you've failed, you need to be able to face your failure, own up to it, and process it emotionally. And you also need to regain your footing and rebuild your emotional strength and resilience before you try to lead others again. If you haven't regained that emotional strength, you're likely to repeat the same mistakes, especially if character and self-leadership issues were at the root of your past problems.

Evolution: Can You Make the Adjustments Needed for Future Success?

After you've identified what went wrong and regathered your strength emotionally, you still have a lot of internal work to do. You need to make the changes in yourself to set you up for future success. Maybe you need to put yourself on a personal growth plan whereby you read a dozen books and attend some conferences. Maybe you need to seek counseling to help you with character issues. Maybe you need to find a mentor. Maybe you need to further your education. Maybe you need greater accountability. You need to figure it out and make necessary adjustments. If you're not willing and able to do that, you probably should not step back into leadership.

Once you're done working on yourself, you still need to do a lot of work with others. You need to earn respect and rebuild trust with people. When you are leading others, you have relational "change" in your pocket that allows you to lead. As FedEx founder Fred W. Smith observed, "Leadership is getting people to work for you when they are not obligated." As long as you have change in your pocket, people will work for you. Every good decision, every win for the team, every positive relational connection with team members cre-

> **"Leadership is getting people to work for you when they are not obligated."**
> —*Fred W. Smith*

ates additional change. Adding change takes time. Every bad decision, every loss, every relational fumble takes away change. Losing change occurs more quickly than earning it.

Some people use up their change slowly. Others lose every bit of it in a single action. If you failed as a leader and lost your position, it was because you ran out of change. The last thing you did wrong may not have been the worst thing you did. Whether you were aware of it or not, it was the thing you did after you had run out of change.

If you desire to lead again, you will need to rebuild trust and earn back relational change. Consultant and former executive of *Fortune* 50 companies Michael Winston asserts, "In every major study on practices of effective leaders, trust in the leader is essential if other people are going to follow that person over time. People must experience the leaders as believable, credible, and trustworthy. One of the ways trust is developed—whether in the leader or any other person—is through consistency in behavior. Trust is also established when words and deeds are congruent."

The process of building trust begins with being honest and transparent about your weaknesses, frailties, and mistakes. People don't expect their leaders to be perfect, but they do expect them to be honest. If you understand your humanness, can learn to accept it, and are open about it, you're in a position to ask people's forgiveness. That's where the trust-building process starts. Many people will never trust you until you ask forgiveness. Some won't trust you even then, but if you're honest and humble about your failure, ask forgiveness, try to make amends, and demonstrate a willingness to change, you've done what you can to move forward. You have no control over whether others forgive you or trust you again. You can only do everything in your power to earn trust from the people you work with. Just be sure that if you regain their trust, you move forward with integrity and don't willingly violate it again.

6. Why Do Some Leaders Fail to Have a Successor?

It's been my observation that there are two main reasons organizations don't have successors. The first is that some leaders simply fail to plan for succession. Some people don't like contemplating the end of the leadership road for themselves, so they simply refuse to think about it. They act as though they will live and lead forever, and they either die while still holding on to their positions or get pushed out once they are no longer effective.

I once heard of a leader who founded an organization and adamantly refused to create a succession plan. When other leaders in his organization pushed him to do it, he dug his heels in. He said he didn't want anyone else to take credit for his accomplishment. He wanted the organization to die with him. I find that to be very selfish.

When organizations fail to have a successor, it's usually not because the leader doesn't want one. More often it's because one of the following happens:

- **The organization doesn't accept the new leader.** Sometimes the people in an organization are so entrenched in old thinking that they won't allow a new person to lead them.
- **The new leader doesn't like the organization.** Sometimes there isn't a good fit, and it's not discovered until the new leader takes the reins.
- **The new leader doesn't fit the corporate culture.** Every organization has its own culture. If the vision and values of the leader don't match up with those of the organization, there will be a clash.
- **The new leader fails to bring about successful changes.** Sometimes the person chosen to succeed a leader isn't as good as hoped. The failure can occur due to lack of ability, capacity, experience, knowledge, or relational connection.
- **The old guard sabotages the efforts of the new leader.** Any time an organization contains leaders who believe they were passed over in favor of another leader, there is the danger that they may do what they can to make the new leader fail.
- **The old leader sabotages the efforts of the new leader.** Occasionally the person stepping down has a hard time seeing someone else succeed in the position.

There are certainly no guarantees when it comes to succession, yet I believe it is something worth fighting for. The Law of Legacy in *The 21 Irrefutable Laws of Leadership* states, "A leader's lasting value is measured by succession."

> **A leader's lasting value is measured by succession.**

As I write this, I am sixty-seven years old. I don't believe it's time for me to step down from leadership. I think I still have more to give. But I've been thinking about legacy and succession for several years now. It's my desire to build organizations that will survive me and continue to make a difference. I'm working to help the leaders of The John Maxwell Company, the John Maxwell Team, and EQUIP to think ahead. Together we're planning for the day when my run is over and someone else will be better able to add value to people.

7. What Are the Most Important Things a Leader Transitioning Out of a Position Can Do to Ensure the Success of the Person Taking Over the Role?

Bob Russell and Bryan Bucher, authors of *Transition Plan*, liken the succession process to that of passing the baton in a relay race, which I think is an apt description. Here are the points they make on how the two processes are similar. They say,

- The one passing the baton must keep running full steam until the baton is passed.
- The one receiving the baton must start running before he receives it.
- Both runners must remain in the same lane.
- The baton must be passed in a timely fashion.
- If the exchange is handled properly, it's possible to gain a step in the transition instead of losing a step.
- Once the baton is exchanged, the one passing the baton does not run alongside the next runner coaching him, but stops, catches his breath and walks across the infield to cheer for the successor at the finish line.[31]

If you are preparing to pass the leadership baton to a successor, that needs to be your primary focus as a leader. Jack Welch, former CEO of General Electric, was quoted as saying, "From now on, choosing my successor is the most important decision I'll make. It occupies a considerable amount of thought almost every day." He said this in 1991—nine years before his eventual retirement.

If you are thinking about succession, whether because of a transition to another organization or because you believe your time to lead is coming to an end, I believe you, your organization, and your successor will benefit if you proceed in this way:

1. Plan Ahead

As the outgoing leader, you must do your best to prepare yourself, your successor, and your organization for the upcoming transition. It is your responsibility to the people you lead to make the change as smooth as possible.

I learned this the hard way when I left my first leadership position and transitioned to another organization. I was a young leader in my early twenties, and it never occurred to me to plan for a successor. When it became clear to me that my time there was coming to an end and I needed to seek other growth opportunities, I became open to other possibilities. When I got a chance to take a position that would stretch me as a leader and increase my impact, I took it. I did nothing to prepare the organization I left to make the transition. I didn't know I should, and I didn't know how. It wasn't until later, when I saw the organization lose ground from where I'd left it, that it occurred to me that I should have done something.

2. Pick Your Successor

In some organizations you don't get to pick your successor. It's done by another leader or by a board of directors. However, if it is within your power, pick someone who has the potential to take the organization farther than you have. Obviously you want to look for high leadership gifting and strong skills for your industry. But also keep in mind how long the person will have the potential to lead. Russell and Bucher explain that Zenith, a longtime player in consumer electronics, started to decline when its founder handed off the company to a successor who was seventy years old. The man led the company for only two years before stepping down.

Planning for Succession

1. **Prepare yourself.** Many leaders have a hard time letting go of their leadership positions. Some can't handle it emotionally. Some have not prepared financially. Others have not discussed it with their families. Get yourself ready for the idea.

2. **Look for several potential successors.** If you are in a position to pick your successor, look for several people with the potential to replace you. Ideally you would have a pool of people to pick from.

3. **Let the organization know change is on the horizon.** Transitions from one leader to another can be traumatic. Don't spring it on your people. Let them know in plenty of time if it's within your power.

Jack Welch said of his selection process, "I wanted to pick someone young enough to be in the job for at least a decade. While a CEO can have an immediate impact, I always felt people should live with their decisions and especially with their mistakes. I certainly had. Someone with less time might be tempted to make some crazy moves to put his stamp on the company. I've seen too many examples of that."

You probably naturally gravitate to people in your own age bracket. Birds of a feather flock together. If you're my age, don't allow yourself to think of successors of your own generation. Reach down. Look for young leaders with potential. They may not have as much seasoning and experience, but they give the organization a better chance to succeed in the long run.

3. Prepare Your Successor

Focus your efforts on giving the upcoming successor every possible opportunity to take on responsibility, make decisions, and influence the organization *before* the transition. Leadership author Marshall Goldsmith is right when he says, "Succession plans do not develop anyone...only development experiences develop people."

Your goal as a leader should be to work yourself out of a job. Develop your successor as a person and leader. Don't think solely in terms of the job. Try to reproduce yourself. Equip and empower your successor to the point that they can do the job as well as you—and then some. If you give all you can and add it to all they are and bring to the table, you give the person and the organization a good chance to succeed.

> Your goal as a leader should be to work yourself out of a job.

4. Take Care of Any Unfinished Business

If you are leaving an organization on a high note, you probably have a clear perspective on your organization. That means you know where the problems are. No one is in a better position to take care of unfinished business than you are. You have people's respect, and you have the power to solve difficulties for your successor. So why not do that? You can afford to take hits because you have so much credibility. You can create space for your successor to move forward without those difficulties. What a fantastic gift.

5. Say Goodbye

When it's time for you to resign, leave. Few things are more debilitating to a new leader than having his predecessor meddling in the organization and undermining his leadership. Jeffrey Immelt, Jack Welch's successor at General Electric, asserted as he took over as CEO, "The most important thing that Jack can do now, so I can really take the reins, is to leave. I could always call him and ask him for advice. But physically, the business can only have one leader."

When you step down from the leadership of your organization, get out of the way. Let your successor do the job outside of your shadow. As Marshall Goldsmith observed, "The best thing the CEO can do is show integrity on the way out by doing everything possible to ensure that the next CEO is successful." That includes removing yourself so your successor can lead and people in the organization can follow them.

6. Make Yourself Available to Your Successor

Part of saying goodbye is not offering unsolicited advice. However, your successor will appreciate it if you make yourself available when and if they choose to reach out to you. There are things only you can know. You have a perspective that is unique and valuable. Offer it when asked.

I mentioned that when I left my first leadership position, I didn't do a very good job of setting the organization up for success. When I left Skyline after twenty-six years in ministerial leadership, I did a better job. For fourteen years I had planned ahead by developing leaders. I developed the staff, and they became a fantastic team. I also developed my board of directors. While it was true that I did not get to pick my successor, because that would not have been consistent with the bylaws of the organization, I had developed the leaders on the board who did the picking. And when I left my position, I said goodbye. In fact, in my last official act as leader, I told everyone in the organization that when I left that day, I was no longer their leader.

After I made the transition, I tried to do everything in my power to help my successor, Jim Garlow, be successful, including keeping the door open to him any time he wanted to discuss an issue or ask about the history of the organization. I'm always glad to help in any way I can. I love Skyline and its people, and I still want the best for them. When Jim wins, so do the people—and so do I.

8. How Do You Handle Leaving and Breaking the News to a Great Team of Great People Who Came to a Company Because You Asked Them to?

Telling people goodbye can be difficult. Pulitzer Prize–winning columnist Ellen Goodman wrote, "There's a trick to the Graceful Exit. It begins with the vision to recognize when a job, a life stage, a relationship is over—and to let go. It means leaving what's over without denying its validity or its past importance in our lives. It involves a sense of future, a belief that every exit line is an entry, that we are moving on rather than out."

At the time I left Skyline, I was excited about the next phase of life, but I was saddened to leave such great people behind. Some of the key staff had been with me for more than ten years. We had been through a lot together and really cared about one another.

When I made the decision that it was time to leave, I went to my key people and let them know first. I felt that I owed it to them. I also promised to help them in any way I could, and I'm grateful that I was able to follow through on that promise.

When you make a transition, no matter now necessary it is or how well you do it, you will disappoint people you care about. You should not allow that to stop you if it's the right thing to do. Help the people you can. Set your successor up for success. And leave with integrity. You can't expect yourself to do more than that.

9. What Should Be the Legacy of a Successful Leader?

Legacies that matter are connected with people. A hundred years from now all that will matter is the people that you connected with in such a way that you added value and meaning to their lives.

I've spent a large portion of this chapter discussing succession and how to pass the baton of leadership to other leaders. Political commentator Walter Lippmann said, "The final test of a leader is that he leaves behind in others the conviction and will to carry on." Ultimately, if your people can't do it without you, you haven't been successful in raising up other leaders.

We have all heard that "when the student is ready, the teacher appears." I also believe that when the teacher is ready, the student appears. There are people in your world who would be thrilled to learn from you—not just the person who will succeed you in your leadership position, but people in every area of your life.

I believe the greatest legacy a leader can leave is having developed other leaders. Develop them as widely and as deeply as you can. I've spent more than thirty years teaching leadership to leaders from every walk of life and nearly a hundred countries. My organizations have trained millions of leaders in nearly every country. In the last few years, I've begun to personally invest in coaches and speakers who are actively teaching to others the values and principles I embrace. And I'm investing deeply in a handful of leaders in my inner circle.

If you want to leave a legacy, invest in people, and encourage those you develop to pass on everything they learn from you to others who will do the same. People are what matter in this world—not money or fame or buildings or organizations or institutions. Only people.

Many years ago I came across a poem called "The Bridge Builder" by Will Allen Dromgoole. It encapsulates the attitude of legacy-building leaders. It says,

An old man walking a lonesome road,
Came at the evening, cold and gray,
To a chasm vast and wide and steep,
With waters running cold and deep.
The old man crossed in the twilight dim,
The rolling stream had no fears for him;
But he turned when safe on the other side,
And built a bridge to span the tide.

"Old man," said a fellow traveler near,
"you are wasting your strength with building here.
Your journey will end with the passing day,
You never again will pass this way.
You've crossed the chasm, deep and wide—
Why would you build this bridge at eventide?"
The builder lifted his old gray head,
"Good friend, in the path I have come," he said,
"There followeth after me today,
A youth whose feet must pass this way.
The chasm that was nought to me,
To that fair-haired youth may a pitfall be.
He too must cross in the twilight dim—
Good friend, I am building this bridge for him."

Achievement comes to people who are able to do great things for themselves. Success comes when they lead followers to do great things

> **The legacy of successful leaders lives on through the people they touch along the way.**

for them. But a legacy is created only when leaders put their people into a position to do great things without them. The legacy of successful leaders lives on through the people they touch along the way. The only things you can change permanently are the hearts of the people you lead.

Questions Related to Developing Leaders

1. What is the best way to identify leadership potential in others?

2. Is developing leaders more art or science?

3. How do you help people realize the talent within them? How do you help people believe in themselves?

4. How can you help people to achieve their maximum potential when they are in their comfort zone and don't care to leave it?

5. How do you determine how much time to give someone you're developing?

6. When do you release or "give up" on people you are leading, after you've done what you can to help them grow?

7. I have empowered others to lead and come back only to find them without progress and back to doing things the old way. What should I do differently?

8. How can we overcome disappointment when we invest a lot of time, money, work, and heart into our upcoming leaders and they leave?

9. What's the most important thing a person must learn in order to be a leader of leaders?

10. How do you move people into your inner circle?

10

How Can I Develop Leaders?

Everything rises and falls on leadership. If you want to maximize your potential and make a difference, you must become a better leader. That is the key to personal success. If you want to make an impact on your world, you must help others to become better leaders.

Leaders are hard to find, hard to train, and hard to hold. They want to go their own way. But developing leaders is perhaps the most rewarding activity you will ever engage in during your lifetime.

1. What Is the Best Way to Identify Leadership Potential in Others?

If you desire to develop leaders and maximize your impact in this world, the most important question you can ask is how to identify potential leaders. Your success is more dependent on your ability to find and attract good people than on anything else. As successful college football coach and friend Lou Holtz says, "I have coached good players and I have coached bad players. I'm a better coach with good players."

> You will develop good leaders only if you find people who have strong leadership potential.

You will develop good leaders only if you find people who have strong leadership potential. That becomes much easier if you know what you're looking for. Is it possible to find people through trial and error? Sure. Is it effective? Not really.

Have you ever gone looking for an unfamiliar book on unorganized shelves? When you don't know what a book looks like, or you can't remember the title, it can take forever to find it. You pull a book off the shelf. *No, that's not it.* And another. And another. It's tedious work and you might become so discouraged that you give up. But what about when you're looking for a book that you know well? Maybe you remember the distinct color of it or the look of the font on the spine. Even without reading any of the words on the cover, you may be able to identify it with merely a *glance*. It's much easier to find something when you know what you're looking for.

I've looked for people with leadership potential for so long that I have a strong sense of what they look like. When I started out in leadership, that wasn't the case. Now that I've been developing leaders for nearly forty years, it's second nature. I want to share my list of criteria with you so that you too will be able to spot people with leadership potential, recruit them to your team, and begin developing them.

1. Leaders Are Catalysts

Every leader I've ever known has had the ability to make things happen. This is often how they first become recognized. They are like the scrawny withered man in the joke about the lumber camp. The little old man walked into the headquarters of a lumber company in western Canada.

"I'd like a job as a lumberjack," he said.

The foreman tried to talk him out of the idea. After all, he was small. He was old. And he looked too frail and weak for such a demanding job. Undaunted, the old man took up an ax and proceeded to chop down a huge tree in record time.

"That's just astounding," the foreman said. "Where did you learn to fell trees like that?"

"Well," said the old man, "you've heard of the Sahara Forest?"

Replied the foreman, "You mean the Sahara Desert."

"Sure," the old man replied, "that's what it's called now."

When I see someone who can make things happen, it grabs my attention. The ability to make things happen doesn't automatically make a person a leader, but I've yet to meet a leader who didn't have the ability to make things happen.

2. Leaders Are Influencers

Leadership is influence, so of course potential leaders must have the ability to influence other people. Influence is something that cannot be delegated. Every person who wants to lead must possess it, at least to some degree.

As you look at potential leaders and try to gauge their level of leadership, pay attention to whom they influence. Do they influence only their friends and family? That's a pretty low level of influence. If other workers in their department or on their team are influenced, that shows a greater level of ability. When workers outside their department or team follow, that shows even greater promise. If their colleagues follow them, they've developed a pretty high degree of influence. And if they influence you and other people higher than they are in leadership, it indicates quite a bit of ability. These people are already leading and have great promise.

Where Does Influence Come From?

- **Character:** Who they are
- **Relationship:** Whom they know
- **Knowledge:** What they know
- **Communication:** How they connect
- **Passion:** What they feel
- **Experience:** Where they're been
- **Past successes:** What they've done
- **Ability:** What they can do

These factors come together in different quantities to create a leader's recipe for influence. Each person's blend is different, but the result is the same: people follow.

---

3. Leaders Are Relationship Builders

One thing that holds many talented and intelligent people back from being good leaders is a lack of people skills. Someone with weak people skills can become a reasonably good manager, because management is focused on systems and procedures. But nobody without good people skills can be a great leader.

When people on the team don't like someone, they will often try to hurt that person. If they can't cause harm, they will simply refuse to help. If they have no real choice and are *required* to help, they will still be mentally and emotionally against the individual and will hope he or she doesn't succeed. And even if the person does manage to succeed, the victories he or she achieves can feel very hollow and be short-lived. Elevating someone with bad people skills is a recipe for failure.

Good leaders like people and people like them. They work at con-

necting with others and they continually look for opportunities to connect.
That's why you need to select potential
leaders with excellent people skills.

> **Good leaders like people and people like them.**

4. Leaders Are Gatherers

Potential leaders have a quality about them whereby they are always "holding court." Other people are attracted to them. They want to hear what they say. They like being around them because exciting things happen. Often these people are funny and entertaining. They just seem to possess the quality of attraction. People like spending time with them.

When leaders speak, people listen. In a meeting people often wait to hear what leaders have to say. When outgoing people *without* leadership potential speak, nobody listens. They're merely making a speech without an audience. They find it hard to gather people and grab their attention. Whenever I see a person who continually gathers a crowd, I pay attention, because I want to assess whether that person has other qualities that signify leadership potential.

5. Leaders Are Value Adders

Once when I was in Africa, I had the opportunity to go on a safari trip in Kenya. While we were on the plains, I got to meet a Maasai chief. It was a fascinating experience. One of the questions I asked him was "How did you become the chief?" His answer: "I was seen as someone who added value."

That's what all good leaders do—add value. They see their role as leader as a means to help others, not just themselves. They are givers, and they approach life very differently from takers:

Takers ask, "What are others doing for me?"

Givers ask, "What am I doing for others?"

Takers see team members as things that they own.

Givers see team members as people on loan.

Takers consolidate power for personal gain.

Givers share power for the sake of the team.

Can someone lead others without adding value? Certainly. The world is filled with leaders who push others down to raise themselves up, who lead for the power and perks. History is littered with such leaders. But their leadership is fleeting. It adds no value to others. And its impact on the world is negative. Who wants that kind of person on their team?

6. Leaders Are Opportunists

Good leaders see and seize opportunities. They are continually on the lookout for ways to help their organization and advance their team. Leadership authors James M. Kouzes and Barry Z. Posner liken leaders to the settlers who founded the United States or tamed the Western frontier. They write, "Leaders are pioneers—people who are willing to step out into the unknown. They are people who are willing to take risks, to innovate and experiment in order to find new and better ways of doing things."

> "Leaders are pioneers—people who are willing to step out into the unknown."
> —James M. Kouzes and Barry Z. Posner

Leaders, by definition, are out front. They take new territory and others follow them. Great leaders don't merely send others out. They lead the charge. They're more like tour guides than travel agents. They see opportunities, prepare to move forward, and then say, "Follow me." When you see someone who is able to see opportunities and is willing to take good risks, pay attention. You may be looking at a leader.

7. Leaders Are Finishers

Founding father Benjamin Franklin asserted, "I never knew a man that was good at making excuses who was good at anything else." Leaders don't make excuses. They take responsibility, embrace opportunity, and follow through. They live up to their commitments and they can be counted on to finish. To quote the old poem "The Welcome Man" by Walt Mason, which my father often read to me when I was growing up, leaders are the ones who "Deliver the Goods."

Author Kenneth Blanchard says, "There's a difference between interest and commitment. When you're interested in doing something, you do it only when it's convenient. When you're committed to something, you accept no excuses, only results." That's what leaders do. They commit and follow through. They are like Confederate general Jeb Stuart, who used to sign his letters to General Robert E. Lee with the following words: "Yours to count on."

Who Are Your Leaders?

Spend some time looking at the people in your sphere of influence. Have you identified the potential leaders? Whose name would get a check mark for each of the following leadership characteristics?

Catalyst
Influencer
Relationship builder
Gatherer
Value adder
Opportunist
Finisher

Few things are harder than trying to help people without leadership potential to lead. It's like sending ducks to eagle school. It just doesn't work. However, when you pick the right people, developing them is a pleasure. Jack Welch asserted, "If you pick the right people and give them the opportunity to spread their wings—and put compensation as a carrier behind it—you almost don't have to manage them." That's what you're going for.

2. Is Developing Leaders More Art or Science?

Some people want to develop leaders through a highly structured and inflexible system, to try to produce them the way manufacturers punch shapes out of sheets of metal. Other people want the development of their leaders to be entirely organic and without planning, every lesson growing out of the situation at hand. But the truth is that leadership development is both science and art.

ART	SCIENCE
Based on Intuition	Rooted in Fact
Recognizing Talent	Sharpening Talent Through Practice
Inspiring Performance	Evaluating Performance
Developing Relationships	Developing Skills
Identifying Teachable Moments	Implementing a Training Method
Knowing When to Move	Preparing Before the Move

Daniel Goleman has done a lot to help people understand the intuitive side of leadership. His research and writing on emotional intelligence shows that while the qualities traditionally associated with leadership—such as intelligence, technical skills, and determination—are required for success, they tell only part of the story. Effective leaders also possess emotional intelligence, which includes self-awareness, intuition, a capacity for self-leadership, empathy, and people skills. These "softer" skills represent the more creative side of leadership and must be developed as much as the hard skills.

Daniel Goleman says, "It would be foolish to assert that good, old-fashioned IQ and technical ability are not important ingredients of strong leadership. But the recipe would not be complete without emotional intelligence. It was once thought that the components of emotional intelligence were 'nice to have' in business leaders. But now we know that, for the sake of performance, these are ingredients that leaders 'need to have.'"

As you develop leaders, you must identify, nurture, and develop both skill sets. If you're familiar with *The 5 Levels of Leadership*, you know that both permission (the relational aspect of leadership) and production (the results aspect of leadership) are essential to developing influence with people and becoming an effective leader.

3. How Do You Help People Realize the Talent Within Them? How Do You Help People Believe in Themselves?

Napoleon said, "Leaders are dealers in hope." They help people to believe in the vision and in their leadership. But they also help people to believe in themselves. They help people turn hope into action.

Perhaps the most rewarding aspect of leadership is seeing people with hope believe in themselves, develop themselves, and blossom into effective leaders. If you desire to help your people do that, proceed in this way:

Find Evidence That They Want to Grow

You cannot get someone who does not want to grow to embrace personal growth. People must ultimately make that decision for themselves.

I didn't always understand this. There was a time when I believed

> You cannot get someone who does not want to grow to embrace personal growth.

that I could encourage and inspire everyone to take the growth journey with me. I no longer think that. Life is too short to spend time trying to convince people to change and grow while others who *do* desire to grow stand by waiting for you to give them your time and energy. So if you want people to realize their talent, the first thing you've got to do is know the difference between those who want to grow and those who don't. Pour your effort into the best you have, because they will give you the greatest return.

How can you tell who wants to grow? Attitude and effort. People worthy of your time and attention have a learning attitude. They're open to instruction and hungry to grow. They may not yet be convinced that they can reach what you recognize as their potential, but they have the desire. And they are already making an effort to grow. Their efforts may not be strategic. They may not be focused. They may not even be effective. But you can see a spark there. That's all you need to get started.

Identify Their Strengths

The number one problem of people who want to grow but aren't reaching their potential is that they major in their weaknesses. Why is that? I believe it's because that's what they've been taught to do for most of their lives. Think about when you got your report card when you were a child. If you got an A in math and a C-minus in reading, what did your teacher say you needed to work on? Your reading.

That's a good idea when you're dealing with the basics. Everyone needs to learn how to read and do basic math. It's difficult to succeed in life if you can't read a book or look at a bill to see if you're being cheated. However, that's not a good strategy as you get older. If you want to be successful, you need to build on your strengths, not shore up your weaknesses. Nobody pays for average. Nobody purposely hires mediocrity. People pay for excellence. If you're above average at something, you have a shot at becoming excellent at it. If you start out as excellent, you have a chance to be great.

The people you lead may not know what they're good at. Many people grow up with little or no encouragement from the significant adults in their lives. Many people take a convenient job and never give thought to what they could be great at. As a leader you need to help people figure out where they have potential and should grow.

Increase Their Confidence

There are two kinds of people who have confidence, those with a high level of mastery in their area of strength and those who have no knowledge whatsoever and think everything's easy because they've never done anything. Then there's a middle group, which is the largest. These people need your help gaining confidence in themselves.

I help people have confidence by seeing the potential in them, expecting the best out of them, and expressing my belief in them. As people start trying to grow and tackle new challenges, they usually become insecure. Trying to conquer new territory can be scary. That's why you need to lend them your belief. Tell them, "I understand that you're on a journey. This is foreign to you. You may be a bit nervous. That's OK. I believe in you. It's going to be all right. You may not get this on the first try, but you're going to get it. You're a winner and you're going to win. Keep at it."

When you express belief in people, it goes right to their souls. It gives them hope. It stirs their sense of purpose. It helps them be someone they've never been before and do things they've never done before. Knowing that you believe in them causes them to rise up. Is there anything better in the world than having somebody unconditionally love you and believe in you?

Give Them a Place to Practice

Once you've discovered that people want to grow, you've helped them identify their strengths, and you've increased their confidence, you need to provide a place for them to practice what they're learning. Training is good. Mentoring is fantastic. Development is incredible. But if you don't give emerging leaders a place to practice, their knowledge will never become practical experience.

Leadership is so complex that you can't learn it just from a book. You can get ideas. You can open doors mentally. You can understand skill sets, but you won't acquire them and grow if you don't put them into action. People need to make mistakes and learn from them. They need to find out what works for them. They need to work with real people who have strengths and weaknesses, problems and quirks.

Coach Them to Improvement

As people try practicing new skills, you need to allow them to fail safely. People always learn more from their failures than they do from their successes. Walk alongside them to give them security and to help them through the most difficult problems. Share with them where they made mistakes and how they can overcome them. Tell them what to work on. And encourage them to keep trying.

When you first begin to coach them, you may be fairly hands-on. You may stay close to them. As they gain experience, give them more space. It's like helping a child ride a bike. At first you start them out with training wheels. When they start to get a feel for how the mechanics of the bike work, you take the training wheels off, but you stay with them every minute to prop them up. When they gain confidence, you let them go. That first time they balance the bike and pedal, they're excited. They've actually done it! But of course it's only a matter of time before they fall. You're watching them, so you help them get up. You explain what happened. You help them understand how to avoid the same problem, and then watch them ride some more. Eventually, they'll be off riding on their own and won't need you to help them stay upright any longer.

Keep Increasing Their Responsibilities

At this point many leaders make a mistake. As soon as the emerging leader gains a degree of self-sufficiency, they leave that leader alone, grateful that they can finally carry their own weight. It's a relief to have someone who can share the load. But don't stop there. If you have developed a leader who can be successful independently, you will have done more than most other leaders do. And it might feel like you're done. But for the best developers of people, that's not enough. If you continue to work with new leaders and keep increasing their level of responsibility, they will continue to grow and improve.

Your goal should always be to work yourself out of a job. Keep giving your leaders more and more weight to carry. Keep showing them the ropes. Allow them to benefit from your experience until they are capable of doing your job. That takes security on your part. But if you do that, when it comes time for *you* to move up to greater responsibility or move on to a new challenge, you will have people who can step in and take your place. That should always be your goal as a leader.

4. How Can You Help People to Achieve Their Maximum Potential When They Are in Their Comfort Zone and Don't Care to Leave It?

Many people don't have a greater vision for their lives. And it's easy for people, even those who want to grow, to get into a rut and stay in their comfort zone. As a leader you should try to encourage them to move forward and reach for their potential. You're not responsible for their response. Every individual has to take responsibility for that. But you can model growth, encourage them, and try to be a catalyst for positive change. Here's how:

Show Them a Vision for Their Better Future

If people cannot see a better future for themselves, you need to show it to them. Start by asking them questions: If you could be anything you wanted, what would you be? If you could do anything you wanted,

> If people cannot see a better future for themselves, you need to show it to them.

what would you do? If you knew you could not fail, what would you try? See what stirs inside them. Many people have dreams deep inside that need only a bit of encouragement to coax out.

Treat Them Not as They Are, But as They Could Be

I learned this lesson from my dad when I was a child. He treated everyone with kindness and respect, even the people who treated him poorly. And when he had conversations with people within earshot of my brother, my sister, or me, he would speak so highly of us. He talked about us in a way that was so empowering for a child that we literally got a lot of our expectations from those conversations. We wanted to rise to the high level of his treatment of us. I know he did that on purpose, and it was very empowering and confidence building.

If you were to treat the people around you as they could be instead of as they are, how do you think they would respond? If they've been in a rut a long time, they might not rise up right away. You might have to keep speaking positively about them and treating them as people who desire to reach their potential, but I believe that in time most would rise up. And if they don't, what have you lost? Nothing. Give it a try. Speak positively about a better future for them, and they just might try to live up to it.

Set Them Up for a Win

Many times people aren't willing to leave their comfort zone because they are convinced that they cannot win. You can change that by setting them up for success. If you put them in a position where an easy win is almost guaranteed, they can have that winning experience inspire them to move forward.

Here's an example of how you can make this work. If you have someone on your team who you know has the potential to be a fantastic salesman, but who won't get out of his comfort zone, put him in a position to make an easy sale. If you've been working with a client to make a sale and you know that all the barriers have been removed, all the objections have been overcome, and the client is ready to say yes, don't close the sale. Instead say that you have to leave, but ask if you can set up an appointment for the next day. And mention that you're going to bring a colleague with you.

The next day, take that salesman who needs a win to give him confidence. Tell him that you want him to talk to the customer briefly and then ask for the sale. Then watch as the salesman closes the deal. That's the kind of thing that can get someone over the hump and give him or her confidence.

Good developers of leaders don't do everything to benefit themselves. They do what great trainers, coaches, and mentors do. They put the needs of the team ahead of their own. They set people up for success so that they gain confidence and experience. Those qualities are important if you want to see people achieve their potential.

5. How Do You Determine How Much Time to Give Someone You're Developing?

Everybody in your organization needs time and assistance, but that doesn't mean you can help everybody personally. You should be kind and supportive of everyone, but you must pick and choose whom you will develop. If you focus on the top 20 percent of your team, the people with the highest skills and greatest potential to grow, you can ask them to help support and develop the remaining 80 percent.

How to Identify Your Top 20 Percent

Here's what to look for when determining who might be in your top 20 percent:

- **Passion:** Are they excited? Are they positive about the team? Does the vision energize them? Is the work they do fulfilling to them? You don't want to be required to push someone to be developed.
- **Teachability:** Are they growing now? Are they open to new ideas? Are they humble and willing to learn? You want to invest in people who are hungry.
- **Capacity:** What is their potential? Is there plenty of room for growth? Do they possess talent in the area in which you want to develop them? How far could they go if you were to help them?

You may have lots of people worth investing in. If so, don't try to develop more than the top 20 percent. If you spread yourself too thin, people won't get your best. On the other hand, if you judge that you have only one person with potential, invest in him or her.

Once you've identified whom you want to develop, ask them how much time *they* think they need in order to be successful. I think we don't ask these kinds of questions enough. Most of the time, good people will be strategic in their response. Not everyone will be, but good people usually are, because they don't want to just hang out. They want to get things done. They want to achieve something.

If the amount of time they request is appropriate—based on their potential and the amount of time you have—give it to them, but make it convenient to you. Ask them to fit into your schedule and travel to you. And when you do get together, make the most of that time. Make it count.

6. When Do You Release or "Give Up" on People You Are Leading, After You've Done What You Can to Help Them Grow?

Many leaders find it difficult to know when to stop investing in someone they once believed in. Some leaders give up too soon. Others hang on to someone way too long, hoping that person will get back on track.

I believe it's OK to release people if one of these things happens:

You've Given Them the Chance to Change But They Haven't

When you've given people a clear pathway to change, meaning that you've made it clear to them *how* they need to change, you've explained *why* they need to change, and you've given them all the resources that make it *possible* for them to change, yet they still do not change, you need to stop investing in them.

When I started my career, I did quite a bit of counseling with people. I found it very frustrating. When people had a problem, I often could see a clear solution, and all I wanted to do was lay out a course of action for them to take and then wait for them to follow it. But what usually happened was that they came in to talk about the problem, but then didn't actually do anything about it. The next time I saw them, they would tell me about the same problem again. I discovered that many people cared more about being heard and understood than about changing and growing, and there was little I could do about it.

That's not the case for a leader. Not only *can* I offer a course of action for someone to take in order to grow, I'm *expected* to do that for anyone I develop or mentor. When I do, the person can choose to follow my advice or not. And if he or she decides not to follow my direction, I can choose not to give him or her any more of my time. Why should I continue to invest in someone who doesn't want to follow my direction and grow? Why should you?

They Have Broken Trust

When people you're investing in break trust with you, it's time to stop giving them your time and energy. It's been said that if you can't trust everything a person says, you can't trust anything they say. If someone isn't trustworthy anymore, they've violated the relationship. There's no good way to move forward.

You Realize You Would Not Hire Them Again Today

Sometimes, when you work with people for a while, you realize that they didn't have the potential you thought you saw in them when you hired them. Maybe you believed in them more than they believe in themselves and they never rise to your expectations. Maybe they were in an unusually good season when you met them. Or maybe you were mistaken about the talent and skills you thought you saw.

No matter which of these things might be true, the gist is that you now know them better, and you may have come to realize that if you were hiring someone today to fill their role, you would not pick them. If that's true, it's time to stop investing in them, because you've discovered it's a dead end. You can't make people into something they're not. It's time to move on and give your time and energy to someone else who can help the team.

7. I Have Empowered Others to Lead and Come Back Only to Find Them Without Progress and Back to Doing Things the Old Way. What Should I Do Differently?

When I first started hosting conferences to teach leadership and help people learn to lead, I felt a lot of pressure to try to make people succeed, but I knew it wasn't working for everyone. I watched some people soar. But I could see that others were wasting their time because they didn't make any changes and they led others no better than they had before the conference.

That weighed on me tremendously. I kept thinking, *I've got to change these people.* Back then I naïvely thought it was within my power to change people. In some cases I wanted success for them more than they wanted it for themselves.

With time and experience, I of course realized that I can't change anybody else. People have to change themselves through their choices. The only

> I can't change anybody else. People have to change themselves through their choices.

thing I can do is create a positive environment that encourages growth and change.

If there are people in your organization or on your team who aren't learning, growing, and changing, and you've not yet created an environment that promotes growth, try doing the following:

Treat High Achievers as Partners Rather Than Employees

One of the most positive things you can do for your high achievers is close the gap between them and you. One of the ways to do that is to treat your top talent as partners. Your working relationship should look more like a strategic alliance than like a traditional employment arrangement.

What does that mean? It means that as the leader, you're not withholding information from your team to maintain an advantage. You're asking for advice. You're listening as much as or more than you're talking. You include your team in the formation of the vision. You share decision making. You work together with them in everything, rather than handing down assignments.

If you do this consistently, you will see exponential growth in your best people, because they will learn how you think. You will also find that people start carrying the weight of responsibility and volunteer to take on challenges rather than having them assigned to them.

Stay Ahead of Your Strongest Players

You cannot set the tone for the environment if you don't stay ahead of your strongest team members. This doesn't mean that you have to know everything or that you have to lead the pack in every category. I have many people on my team who know more than I do in certain areas. But when it comes to leadership, I work to remain the strongest on the team.

This desire to stay ahead of my best people drives me to keep growing and learning. As leaders creating a positive environment for growth, we must continue to grow, read, research, and interact with other organizations and leaders to remain on the cutting edge. If we do that, we will be able model creative thinking, emotional security, and servant leadership for others.

Reward Achievers Financially

I've found that the best people in my organization have already made the transition from seeking success to striving for significance. They are working for fulfillment, not finances. However, I have always made it a point to reward my top talent financially as a statement of my appreciation. I never want finances to be a distraction or a thorn in my people's side. If they're paid well, they can focus on the things that really matter.

Invest in Achievers Relationally

When people reach a certain level of achievement, the thing they most value is time with someone who's ahead of them and can help them forward through life. They desire a good relationship.

Mentor your best people. Give them time one-on-one. Give them access to you and build a developmental relationship. Your most talented people have a strong desire to learn and grow. Feed that desire. And encourage them to engage in this same process with people who are behind them and coming up.

Stretch High Achievers Continually

A sure sign that someone is a high achiever is that they want to be challenged. That's always true of top talent. If you have exceptional people on your team, you need to be continually thinking of ways to challenge them. You need to find new horizons for them to shoot for. Don't allow them to get bored, because if they do, they'll get restless and start looking for other opportunities.

As a leader, I'm responsible for creating an environment where my people can learn and grow and be successful. I can cheer them on, give them resources, and train them. I am responsible for giving the best of myself—but not their response. I've had people in whom I've made a significant investment keep coming back to me and saying, "You didn't help me enough. You need to help me more. I need more of your time." They weren't taking responsibility for their own success.

It's a mystery to me why one person will thrive in such an environment and another won't. Two people will read one of my books or hear me speak. One will go out and change his or her life forever. The other will walk away disappointed. The same book, same conference, and same speaker can lead to totally different responses.

Give people your best, but don't carry the weight of their choices. Don't carry the weight of the results. Help whom you can, and allow the others to find another environment or another leader who can help them.

8. How Can We Overcome Disappointment When We Invest a Lot of Time, Money, Work, and Heart into Our Upcoming Leaders and They Leave?

To be honest, you don't get over it. The best you can do is try to gain wisdom from it. Loss is the beginning of wisdom. The pain and hurt of having great people leave you makes you give greater attention to the process, especially if you have invested heavily in the people who leave. Try to wish them well, and don't allow yourself to get bitter.

You may be tempted to stop investing in people as a result. Don't give up the process. I'll tell you why: the only thing worse than developing people and losing them is not developing them and keeping them. If you stop developing people, your organization or team has started to decline. And it will continue to decline while other organizations pass you by. The best thing you can do is learn from your experiences and do your best to hold on to your strongest people going forward.

We are living and leading in a world of free agents. People leave for a variety of reasons. You may or may not be able to keep all your best people. They may leave for reasons that have nothing to do with you. But do your best to keep them. Don't give them reasons to leave. Make your purpose larger than you. Give them every opportunity to work for significance, not just success. Pay them as well as you can. Help them grow. And create a great environment that makes it very difficult for people to leave. That's all you can do.

9. What's the Most Important Thing a Leader Must Learn in Order to Be a Leader of Leaders?

There's only one way to lead leaders. Become a better leader yourself. Good leaders do not follow poor ones. People naturally follow leaders stronger than themselves. That's the Law of Respect from *The 21 Irrefutable Laws of Leadership.*

When leaders get together, they naturally size each other up. They test one another. They challenge one another. Some people do it with humor, others by trying to get people off their game. Sometimes it's playful. Other times it's not. But if you put a bunch of leaders in a room, they'll be able to tell you which of them is the strongest. Put non-leaders in the room, and they won't even be in the game.

So if you want to be a leader of leaders, you will need to earn the right. You will need to achieve success first. The higher the capacity of the leaders you desire to lead, the bigger the success you need to have in your history. You'll need to keep raising your leadership capacity. You'll need to make growth a major goal and dedicate yourself to it. And you'll also have to keep your ego in check. If you have a compulsive need to be the alpha dog, the other top dogs won't want to work with you.

10. How Do You Move People into Your Inner Circle?

Most of the people who are in my inner circle have arrived there because they've proven themselves or because I saw where they could add value. Most of the time, people determine their own longevity. Many former inner circle members stayed with me for a season and then decided to move on to other things. A handful of them have remained with me for over twenty years. Change is fine. The main question you must ask yourself is whether the inner circle is better today than it was yesterday.

Before I think about moving someone into my inner circle, I consider the following:

1. Time

I don't put someone into my inner circle without having history with that person. It's just too risky. You need to know someone's character before you allow them to handle important parts of your world. It also takes time to develop the relationship. I tend to make quick judgments about people. I'm also very trusting. So I have to fight the urge to bring someone in too quickly.

2. Trust

For your inner circle to be effective, you must totally trust the people in it. You can't be asking about their motives. If you do, you'll always keep up your guard, and they won't be able to help you the way they need to.

3. Experience

To be in my inner circle, people need to have experience—not just professional experience, but life experience. I believe people need seasoning to make good decisions. For that reason I don't want anyone too young. There's no one currently in my inner circle younger than his or her late thirties.

4. Success

For someone to be in my inner circle, they need to have achieved some success. They need to have proven themselves. They must possess the proven ability to add value to me and the organization. Being asked into the inner circle isn't their chance to "make it." They need to already have some wins in their résumé to be considered for the inner circle. You get in because you're good, not because you have the potential to be good.

5. Compatibility

Life is too short to work every day with people you don't like. There isn't anyone in my inner circle I'm not compatible with. The group has a variety of personality types and a variety of skills and gifting. But we're all on the same page and all get along great. Every day of my life I tell the people in my inner circle that I love them, and I really mean it.

> Life is too short to work every day with people you don't like.

6. Capacity

A person can bring every one of those other things to the table, but if they don't have capacity, they cannot be in my inner circle. I move fast, I get a lot done, and I expect the people on my team to do the same. Neither I nor the rest of the team has time to wait around for someone who's lagging behind. We need for people to keep up, not to be trying to help them catch up. We can work together only if we're all together.

Finding Your Inner Circle

What qualities will you require for people in your inner circle? Is your list the same as mine? Or do you require something different? Think about it. Then start building your own inner circle. Your goal should be to surround yourself with a small group of people who love you for who you are, possess the ability to add value to you, have a sense of loyalty to you, and desire to help you achieve your purpose. You, in return, need to help them achieve theirs.

When I turned forty, I realized that my success would depend on the leaders closest to me on my team. That's when I started to invest heavily in individual leaders in my organization and identify who would be able to best help me and the organization. In the decade and a half since then, I've always tried to give my best to my inner circle.

Every leader's inner circle is a blessing or a curse. Every person on your team carries two buckets: one contains gasoline and the other water. When there's a fire, they use one bucket or the other on it. The higher you are in an organization, the later you are on the scene. Who gets the hot issues first? Your inner circle. If they like throwing gasoline instead of water on a fire, you're toast. That will blow up the organization. Every person in my inner circle cares about me and the organization. Every one of them uses the water bucket when fire breaks out.

My inner circle has changed a lot since I was forty. I've changed organizations more than once. People have come and gone. Many leaders believe and hope that their inner circle will always remain the same. I mentored one leader whose core group was five leaders. "We're going to stay together forever," he told me. I knew he'd be lucky to still have one by the end of his leadership tenure.

Now that I'm in my late sixties, I value my inner circle even more than I have before. We lead together. We laugh together. We cry together. We try to make a difference together. I can't imagine life without them.

If you have not yet developed an inner circle, I strongly encourage you to do so. Some members will eventually leave you. Some will probably hurt you. All of them will help you. And you will never regret bringing them together. When you're my age, you will look back at your time with them as one of your greatest joys.

Conclusion

If you approached this book with questions about leadership, I hope I was able to answer some of them for you. As you learn more about leadership and develop as a leader, you will probably find that the questions never end. I've been studying leadership for more than forty years and I'm still looking for answers to new questions. It's at the heart of my continued growth as a leader and as a human being.

Just as importantly, I hope you have a new appreciation for questions and have begun to make asking questions a regular discipline in your life. Every day I still ask myself the same questions I discussed in chapter two. They continue to guide my leadership and help me to be accountable for the gifts and advantages I have been given.

And the questions I ask my team have been indispensible to my success as a leader. No leader can know everything, be an expert in everything, or do everything. It takes a team to be successful. By asking questions, I harness the horsepower of every member of my team, and together we pull the weight of the organizations.

As you move forward, remember that good leaders ask great questions. They may not always know the answers, but they are made better simply by asking them.

Notes

1. Marilyn vos Savant, "Ask Marilyn," *Parade*, July 29, 2007, 8.
2. Bobb Biehl, *Asking Profound Questions* (Mount Dora, FL: Masterplanning Group International, 1996).
3. 1 Kings 3:7, New International Version.
4. Larry King, *How to Talk to Anyone, Anytime, Anywhere* (New York: Three Rivers Press, 1994), 53.
5. Question, Dictionary.com, *Online Etymology Dictionary*, Douglas Harper, historian, accessed August 22, 2013, http://dictionary.reference.com/browse/question.
6. Rick Warren, "3 Ways of Thinking that are Holding You Back," accessed August 30, 2013, http://pastors.com/3-ways-of-thinking-that-are-holding-you-back/.
7. Jeff Chu, "A New Season at Apple," *Fast Company*, February 2014, 57.
8. Ibid, 55.
9. Proverbs 18:16, New International Version.
10. Stephen R. Covey, "Foreword," in Kevin Hall, *Aspire: Discovering Your Purpose Through the Power of Words* (New York: William Morrow, 2009), xii.
11. Don Yaeger, "Lessons from Sports: Nolan Ryan's Longevity," *Success*, accessed September 5, 2013, http://www.success.com/articles/1114-lessons-from-sports-nolan-ryan-s-longevity.
12. Charles T. Horngren and V. "Seenu" Srinivasan, "Memorial Resolution: Thomas W. Harrell," *Stanford Report*, March 9, 2005, accessed September 6, 2013, http://news.stanford.edu/news/2005/march9/memlharr-030905.html.
13. Henry Kimsey-House, Karen Kimsey-House, Phillip Sandahl, and Laura Whitworth, *Co-Active Coaching: Changing Business, Transforming Lives, Third Edition* (Boston: Nicholas Brealey Publishing, 2011), 33–47.
14. Art Mortell, "How To Master The Inner Game of Selling," Vol. 10 No. 7.
15. Eugene B. Habecker, *The Other Side of Leadership: Coming to Terms with the Responsibilities that Accompany God-Given Authority* (Wheaton, IL: Scripture Press, 1987).

16. Stephen Covey, "Books: The 7 Habits of Highly Effective People. Habit 7: Sharpen the Saw," accessed August 11, 2013, https://www.stephencovey.com/7habits/7habits-habit7.php.

17. Charles Swindoll, "Sitting in the Light," *Day by Day with Charles Swindoll* (Nashville: Thomas Nelson, 2005), 170.

18. Jim Collins, *Good to Great: Why Some Companies Make the Leap…and Others Don't* (New York: Harper Business, 2001), 22.

19. Proverbs 10:17, New Living Translation.

20. J. Oswald Sanders, *Spiritual Leadership: Principles of Excellence for Every Believer* (Chicago: Moody Bible Institute, 1967), 27.

21. Leonard Ravenhill, "Prayer," accessed 24 October 2013, http://www.lastdaysministries.org/Mobile/default.aspx?group_id=1000040809&article_id=1000008602.

22. Thomas Clapper, " 'Mr. Meek' at Home," *Racine Journal Times*, February 20, 1942, 8.

23. Author unknown.

24. Ecclesiastes 3:1, New International Version.

25. Del Jones, "Music Director Works to Blend Strengths," *USA Today*, October 27, 2003, accessed September 25, 2013, http://usatoday30.usatoday.com/educate/college/careers/profile9.htm.

26. Jenna Goudreau, "The Secret Power of Introverts," *Forbes*, January 26, 2012, accessed September 25, 2013, http://www.forbes.com/sites/jennagoudreau/2012/01/26/the-secret-power-of-introverts/.

27. Mike Myatt, "15 Ways to Identify Bad Leaders," *Forbes*, October 18, 2012, accessed November 15, 2013, http://www.forbes.com/sites/mikemyatt/2012/10/18/15-ways-to-identify-bad-leaders/.

28. Jacquelyn Smith, "How to Deal with a Bullying Boss," *Forbes*, September 20, 2013, accessed November 15, 2013, http://www.forbes.com/sites/jacquelynsmith/2013/09/20/how-to-deal-with-a-bullying-boss/.

29. M.G. Siegler, "Eric Schmidt: Every 2 Days We Create As Much Information As We Did Up to 2003," *TechCrunch*, August 2, 2010, accessed November 29, 2013, http://techcrunch.com/2010/08/04/schmidt-data/.

30. Jeanne Meister, "Job Hopping is the 'New Normal' for Millennials: Three Ways to Prevent a Human Resource Nightmare," *Forbes*, August 14, 2012, accessed November 29, 2013, http://www.forbes.com/sites/jeannemeister/2012/08/14/job-hopping-is-the-new-normal-for-millennials-three-ways-to-prevent-a-human-resource-nightmare/.

31. Bob Russell and Bryan Bucher, *Transition Plan: 7 Secrets Every Leader Needs to Know* (Louisville, KY: Ministers Label, 2010), 45–48.

Index

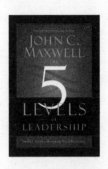
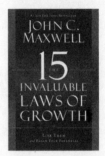

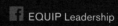
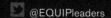